THE
FINANCIAL SECTOR
OF THE AMERICAN
ECONOMY

edited by
STUART BRUCHEY
UNIVERSITY OF MAINE

A GARLAND SERIES

THE EFFECTS OF MONEY, INFLATION AND INTEREST RATES ON RESIDENTIAL INVESTMENT

ANDY DANIELL

GARLAND PUBLISHING, Inc.
New York & London / 1994

Library of Congress Cataloging-in-Publication Data

Daniell, Andy.
  The effects of money, inflation and interest rates on residential
investment / Andy Daniell.
    p.   cm. — (The financial sector of the American economy)
  Includes bibliographical references and index.
  ISBN 0–8153–1762–X (alk. paper)
  1. Investments—United States—Econometric models.   2. Mone-
tary policy—United States—Econometric models.   3. Inflation
(Finance)—United States—Econometric models.   4. Interest rates—
United States—Econometric models.   I. Title.   II. Series.
HG4910.D36   1994
332.63'24—dc20
                                                            94–21347
                                                            CIP

Printed on acid-free, 250-year-life paper
Manufactured in the United States of America

To my parents, Bob and Yvonne, and my wife, Tina

CONTENTS

PREFACE

The research underlying this book, completed in late 1991, took one main approach in looking at real residential fixed investment to study and update a number of areas of interest in macroeconomic and monetary theory. As opposed to an orthodox partial equilibrium demand estimation, a vector autoregressive study of the output measure was performed in an empirical environment common to conventional business cycle investigations. Topics addressed with the results of this work included the place of residential investment in historical business cycles, and the effect of financial deregulation on residential investment and the business cycle. Issues of a more general nature examined included re-testing recent theories which empirically dismiss a causal role for monetary policy and interest rates in real economic fluctuations.

Since the completion of this work, only one of the above topics has been re-visited in the literature. Two articles of particular interest are Bernanke and Blinder (1992) and Kashyap, et al. (1993). The conclusions of their research stand in contrast to that of Sims (1980b). Sims uses money aggregates to represent monetary policy in a series of vector autoregressions. His main conclusion was that monetary policy has no effect on real output[1]. The common theme of the Bernanke and Blinder and Kashyap articles is that monetary policy is thought to affect the economy through bank loans and not through the standard money or bank deposit avenue. The assumption that bank loans and open market securities are not perfect substitutes to either the banks or the businesses who borrow is also common to both papers[2]. Bernanke and Blinder draw from McCallum (1983) who argues that interest rates may be a more appropriate means of discerning Federal Reserve monetary policy intentions than are monetary aggregates. Their interest rate choice is the federal funds rate and they provide empirical support that it is a proxy for Federal Reserve policy. Their results show that monetary policy does affect the real economy.

Kashyap and his co-authors add to this credit view of monetary transmission by showing that restrictive monetary policy reduces future real activity via a reduction in loans. They are able to counter arguments that reductions in loans are responses to output or to reductions in money demand.

These articles were more successful than this book in reversing the conclusions of Sims. They were able to accomplish these results by using both a different Theory and statistical approach than those employed in this book. Since the completion of the study reported in this book, however, no documented work has attempted to directly challenge the implications of Fama's (1982) theory set forth in the empirical work of Litterman and Weiss (1985) and Lawrence and Siow (1985). These works removed a causal role from interest rates relative to business cycles activity[3]. This book remains the most successful challenge to these theories and their empirical support. Also, nothing has been advanced beyond this work concerning real residential investment and its place (and magnitude of its importance) in business cycles.

Because of the number of topics covered in this book and the amount of time which has elapsed between its completion and publication, there are areas which deserve further research. Among these research possibilities is the incorporation of residential investment's behavior into Keynesian, neo-classical and real business cycle theories. Finally, more complete research is needed regarding the effects of financial deregulation on residential investment and how this translates into deregulatory effects on the entire real economy. The results of the effects of deregulation found in chapter 5 are very interesting but were limited to a small number of observations.

NOTES

1. *Sims' theory is discussed in more detail in chapter 2, pp. 16-18.*

2. *The lack of substitutability between bank loans and securities is due, in part, to asymmetrical information enjoyed by banks about their customers.*

3. *These articles are discussed fully in chapter 2, pp. 19-23 and chapter 4, p. 62.*

INTRODUCTION

This book reports the results of an examination of a component of disaggregated total fixed investment, residential fixed investment (RI). The goal is to determine empirically whether RI is affected by money and/or interest rates. This will serve as an indirect method of examining whether the general business cycle is affected by monetary policy or interest rates. This is done using an atheoretical statistical technique which considers potential simultaneous or mutual causality among the variables, vector autoregressions (VARs).

Residential fixed investment is classified by the Commerce Department as an aggregate measure of output whose cyclical movements consistently lead those of the overall business cycle. It has long been considered as a primary contributor to the cyclical patterns of the overall economy. Empirical studies devoted to establishing the existence and magnitude of monetary policy and interest rate effects on RI and of RI's concomitant effect on the total economy, though, have been limited. This book outlines an empirical investigation of RI in detail which has not been undertaken heretofore.

A voluminous body of empirical literature, which includes both partial and general equilibrium approaches, exists to support the view that the other component of total fixed investment, business fixed investment (BFI), is not responsive to either the rate of interest (real or nominal) or monetary policy (e.g. Eisner, 1978 and Lawrence and Siow, 1985). No similar body has been generated exclusively, however, for residential fixed investment. Some papers have made note of the fact that residential fixed investment appears to be responsive to the interest rate (and more so than other components of GNP). However, these papers have been using partial equilibrium structural models that fail to incorporate possible simultaneous determination. These investigations have involved the estimation of housing demand functions and have attempted to estimate income, price or interest rate elasticities. The approach taken in these articles is micro in nature. This book describes a work which is macro in nature and looks to document general cyclical behaviors and relationships between RI and other macro variables.

Although some empirical analyses have considered total fixed investment (e.g. Sims, 1981 and Fama and Gibbons, 1982), this would not have allowed for an accurate portrayal of the relationships to be examined here. It has been empirically documented (including recent articles such as Akhtar and Harris,1987 and Kahn,1989) that the two components of fixed investment react differently to variables such as interest rates, income or output. Therefore, applying the statistical implications of total fixed investment individually to either of its two components would be erroneous.

Therefore, one of the main objectives of the research behind this book was to document the business cycle properties of RI and its relationship to monetary policy, inflation, interest rates and output. The results document formally RI as a leading impulse to the business cycle. Other important conclusions center around the recent business cycle theories regarding the limited efficacy of monetary policy (e.g. Sims' theory of post-war business cycles) and new evidence regarding the lack of a documented causality from interest rates to fluctuations in real economic activity (e.g. the Fama-Litterman-Weiss hypothesis). Using RI provides a unique way of re-examining these theories as it is an aggregate which reaches it's cyclical peaks and troughs prior to the general trade cycle. These hypotheses were originally formulated and tested using aggregates or indices which coincide with or lag the general business cycle. A leading series provides a valuable test of these theories' controversial conclusions.

This research helps to re-establish firmly, within these new theoretical frameworks, a link between interest rates and real economic activity. The continuity and stability of all results are re-tested for the era after the deregulation of the financial and banking sectors of the economy. The results contained in the book help to extend the macroeconomic knowledge of RI to the depth of that known currently for other major output aggregates (such as gross national product, business fixed investment and industrial production).

FIGURES

TABLES

The Effects of
Money, Inflation
and Interest Rates
on Residential
Investment

I

Overview And Outline

The U.S. Department of Commerce, Bureau of Economic Analysis defines residential fixed investment (RI) as the expenditures on the construction of single and multifamily dwellings plus those on additions, alterations and major replacements of the same and final mobile home sales. For the period 1950.1-1990.3, RI has, on average, accounted for a 5.2 percent share of gross national product (GNP). Figure 1.1 shows real residential investment in billions of 1982 dollars for the period listed above. RI is characterized by both large seasonal and cyclical fluctuations. Its volatility (in terms of percent movements from quarter to quarter) is much more severe than that experienced by other major aggregates such as GNP, personal income or even business fixed investment. These extreme changes in value over such short periods of time are what allow a relatively small component of total output to influence the cyclical nature of the national economy. For example, in the 3rd quarter of 1978 RI accounted for a 5.75 percent share of GNP, in the 3rd quarter of 1982 it accounted for only a 3.17 percent share and in the 3rd quarter of 1986 it accounted for a 5.40 percent share.

Although it was the purpose of this research to test empirically the theory that RI is a force behind the business cycle, it could not be assumed that the general business cycle itself, or other components of the cycle, do not have reciprocal effects on RI. Also, it could not be assumed that RI did not have reciprical effects on money, interest rates or inflation. Allowing for the possibility of joint determination is very

3

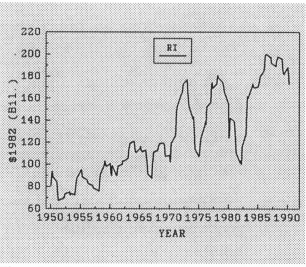

Figure 1.1 Real RI.

important for valid empirical results when there is not strict one-way causality from the independent to the dependent variable. Given this, and uncertain as to the causality flows, an interdependent system of equations was needed to document accurately the behaviors which were of concern. The statistical procedure chosen was vector autoregressions (VARs).

Much like a system of simultaneous equations, VARs allow for mutual causality and feedback among variables. For the purposes here, however, VARs will have an advantage over standard simultaneous equation systems. The advantage is that in a VAR all variables can be considered endogenous and feedback effects do not have to be known before the model can be specified and estimated. That is, the model allows the data to determine exogeneity and assumptions can be kept to a minimum. VARs are discussed in more detail in Chapter 3.

The usefulness of VARs as the estimation technique was further enhanced by the fact that the two main contemporary business cycle theories which this book re-tests were built around results from VARs. Monetarists researchers had always been able to show empirically that changes in monetary aggregates lead changes in economic activity and this was all they needed to support their theories. The ex ante real rate of interest was always mentioned (along with the more direct real balance effect) by monetarists as one of the few likely transmission mechanisms. However, several economists, using VARs as their statistical technique and new theoretical approaches regarding the expectations component of the nominal interest rate, recently have shown that various macro variables are either less responsive to the interest rate (e.g. Lawrence and Siow, 1985), or monetary policy (e.g. Kydland and Prescott, 1990), or both than previously thought. Others have raised questions about money's exogeneity or found that money itself has little influence on the real rate of interest (Sims, 1980b and Litterman and Weiss, 1985). Of course, the real interest rate is of concern in most theoretical models of macro variables. If money does not affect the real interest rate this implies that money does not affect the economy unless it does so through the more controversial mechanism of real balance effects.

The vast majority of business cycle research heretofore has empirically investigated GNP or some other coincidental series (e.g. industrial production). There is, however, a strong case to be made for the belief that if money and/or interest rates affect the economy as a whole it would be through series whose peaks and troughs lead those of the overall business cycle, such as RI. In relatively calm economic times (like the quarter century after the Second World War), the relationships between money and interest rates to the overall economy through leading series may be systematic and stable enough to allow fairly accurate conclusions to be drawn without any consideration having been given to the leading series. In the past two decades, however, the stability and continuity of the chain of events from money to aggregate economic activity may have deteriorated and become very convoluted from an empirical standpoint. Events over the last 20 years such as numerous oil shocks, periods of high inflation, nominal and real interest rates moving in opposite directions throughout much of the seventies, the dramatic disinflation of the early eighties and dramatic changes in the operating procedures of the Federal Reserve, may now make it important to study each link in the chain of a business cycle. Given this, an examination of money's effect on RI becomes even more important. Therefore, the failure to have considered the possibility of the link from money and interest rates through a leading series would seem to undercut the recent studies which have removed a causal role for money and interest rates in real economic cycles.

Because of the strong relationship believed to exist between the rate of interest and both residential investment and the money supply, the presumption has been that a relationship exists between the latter two variables. However, virtually no research has been conducted on the question. Residential investment seems both theoretically and empirically tied to long term rates, while changes in money most systematically affect short term rates. Also, it has been shown both empirically[1] and theoretically that at least some portion of residential investment's historical sensitivity to the rate of interest has been due to financial disintermediation, and thus only indirectly to changes in money supply growth[2]. Given these two facts, it is not clear that a relationship between RI and money exists. This issue needs to be examined. Also, these facts point to the factors that need to be considered in undertaking the examination.

Most of the business cycle investigations and many of the econometric techniques that have evolved over the past decade through the line of business cycle research have not been applied to RI. For the sake of completeness in business cycle research, all large cyclical components of the economy should be compared against one another and should be re-evaluated for each technique which holds the potential to change previous conclusions regarding the relationships between these components. For money, interest rates (real and nominal), inflation (expected and actual), GNP, BFI, and industrial production, this has been done. The goal of the research behind this book was to bring the empirical knowledge concerning RI up to the level of detail currently known for other aggregate time series. One of the main objectives was to document the cyclical relationships of RI to money, inflation and interest rates.

A more specific focus of the research was to examine the possible change in any of these relationships since the onset of the deregulation of the financial and banking sectors of the economy. This deregulation culminated with the passage of the Depository Institutions Deregulation and Monetary Control Act of 1980. Three articles which test for this change regarding the rate of interest (Akhtar and Harris, 1987, Kahn, 1989 and Pozdena, 1990) reach opposing conclusions. No article to date has directly tested for this possible change relative to monetary policy.

As is evident in the discussion of previous works on this topic, (Chapter 2 below), the work herein addressed several existing gaps in the literature. The direct effect of money on RI (in both pre and post-deregulation settings) has not been examined. Also, the impact of money, long term real and nominal rates, anticipated and realized inflation and aggregate income variables on RI have not been assessed in anything like a simultaneous or a VAR system. Finally, the validity of the Fama-Litterman-Weiss hypothesis relative to RI has not previously been examined.

NOTES

1. After the removal of a linear time trend from each variable, the Pearson correlation coefficient between real residential investment and the federal funds rate is -.4356, between the former and the prime rate -.5709, and between real residential investment and the FHA mortgage rate in the secondary market -.6602.

2. This line of thought is presented below, with statistical support, in chapters 2 and 5.

II

Review Of The Literature

ESTABLISHMENT OF THE IMPORTANCE OF MONEY

This section presents a background of early monetary business cycle research. It is meant to provide a survey of the techniques used by early researchers and more importantly of the conclusions reached and the concomitant significance of the role assigned to money. Further, this section's review serves to highlight the type of economic time series aggregates that have received the overwhelming majority of the researchers' attention in previous business cycle investigations.

Prior to the Keynesian revolution, money and monetary policy were considered to be the primary factors motivating the swings of aggregate economic activity about its trend. Monetary theories of trade cycles were set forth in such influential works as *Business Cycles* (Mitchell, 1913) and "The Business Cycle Largely a 'Dance of the Dollar'" (Fisher, 1923). Friedman and Schwartz (1963b) note that such beliefs had "been rather out of fashion for the past few decades" but were making a comeback around the time of their writing. Friedman and Friedman and Schwartz ushered an important role for money and particularly monetary theories of the business cycle back into popularity in the late 1950's and early 1960's. In articles such as "Money and Business Cycles" (1963b) and their book *A Monetary History of the United States* (1963a), Friedman and Schwartz presented a wealth of data (over 90 years' worth) combined to support both graphically and empirically their view of the role of money, along with insightful and detailed explanations of any anomalies or inconsistencies which appeared between their theory and the data. A brief overview of "Money and Business Cycles" will serve here to take account of the body of monetarist literature which both preceded and followed it.

Friedman and Schwartz compare peaks and troughs in the rate of change in the money stock with peaks and troughs in overall business cycles by indicating the characteristics of the timing relationship between the two (for the years 1871-1960). Data for the years 1871-1907 were semi-annual (due to the lack of availability) and data for the years 1908-1960 were monthly. For each of the more than 20 cycles reported, peaks in the rate of growth of the money stock (currency + adjusted demand and time deposits held by the non-bank public) led the peaks in the overall business cycle by an average of 18 months (with a standard deviation of 7 months), and the trough in the decline in the rate of growth of the money stock led the trough in the overall business cycle by an average of 12 months (with a standard deviation of 6 months). In order to determine whether the most severe movements in the rate of growth of the money stock are paralleled with the most severe movements (from trough to trough and peak to peak) with overall business activity, Friedman and Schwartz performed rank order correlations on the two. The correlation coefficients for the entire sample (1879-1961) were .78 and .77 for the trough to trough and peak to peak measures respectively. For the semi-annual data from years 1879-1907, the numbers were .76 and .79. For the monthly data from years 1907-1961, the same correlation coefficients were .75 and .81. This, of course, suggests that the stronger the change in the rate of growth of money has been in the previous months, the more marked will be the change in general business activity in the current and future months.

Friedman and Schwartz believe that this evidence leaves little doubt that changes in money have preceded changes in general economic activity, and that the relative magnitudes of the changes have moved similarly over time. They admit, however, that this does not guarantee causality over coincidence. In order to substantiate their bid for causality, the authors go through the simple steps that might occur after an increase in money through open market operations to lay a theory under the data. In essence, they have money balances increase through a central bank purchase of bonds. This money is then either held by the public or put into a bank (or kept by the bank if it was the entity that sold the bond). Banks could now create more money through a multiplier process, or either the banks or non-bank public could purchase equities or re-purchase debt issues similar to the ones sold to the central bank. This last process will act to drive up the price of securities and drive down the rate of return on those securities (as will the initial purchase by the central bank). With the interest rate declining, Friedman and Schwartz comment that "business enterprises wishing to engage in capital expansion, house builders or prospective homeowners and consumers - who are potential purchasers of durable consumer goods [p. 61]" could one or all be sparked as potential creators of assets. Through these processes "the initially redundant money balances concentrated in the hands of those first affected by the open market purchases become spread throughout the economy [p.61]." This new money may cause output and the return to factors of production all to increase initially. In this model, though, goods prices will also rise as each economic agent rids itself of its new excess nominal money balances. The key factor here is that what originally appeared to be "redundant money balances", and was therefore released into the economy, was based on an erroneous expectation of future prices (as expectations are sluggish), and as realized future prices erode the value of the remaining money balances, they become insufficient. Outflows of money are then reduced in order to re-stock real money balances and bring them back up to the desired (original) level. This reduction in the outflow of funds reverses the processes which were set in motion by the original increase in the rate of money growth. Cyclical fluctuations in economic aggregates consequently occur. A symmetrical sequence of events (in reverse), the theory says, would hold for declines (either permanent or temporary) in the rate of growth of the money stock (i.e. economic or business activity would first decline and then rise again). A similar theory of how money can (and cannot) affect the output of the economy is presented in Friedman (1968).

Friedman and Schwartz emphasized that this was in no way a complete and concrete theory of the transmission process by which changes in money affect the real economy, but only one possible explanation of how the process could work. Critics have complained that one of the main weaknesses of the monetarist theory is the lack of a thorough explanation of the dynamic mechanism which "spreads" the money balances throughout the economy (Friedman, et al., 1974).

Another charge against the theory is that it involves cyclical fluctuations around an immutable trend with no permanent real effects of money.

The monetarist theory is important as a popular explanation of the cyclical behavior of economic time series aggregates which strongly suggests that there must be an empirical relationship by which money affects the real economy. Although Monetarist do not support a specific transmission mechanism, the effect of ex ante real rates on residential investment is explicitly mentioned as one possibility. While this theory and the research underlying this book have a common aspect (an investigation of whether money can affect movements about trend in macro data), there are also differences. For example, this research is looking at a specific transmission mechanism on a specific macro series and does not necessitate that real changes brought on by money be of an ephemeral nature.

In an article with a similar bent to the previously mentioned Friedman and Schwartz paper, Sims (1972) sets out not only to show that movements in money and income are correlated, but also that while money can be shown to Granger "cause" income the reverse relation does not hold. He does this by employing a new F-test for causality which provides a single test of whether causality is one way or reciprocal. Unidirectional causality, Sims says, is important because "most efficient estimation techniques for distributed lags are invalid unless causality is unidirectional [p. 540]."

Sims makes note of the evidence of the monetarists which shows that money changes tend to lead income changes but says that, without disproof that "money might equally well react passively and very reliably to fluctuations in income [p. 540]," no inference about a one-way directional relationship could be made. The fact that one variable leads another variable and does not react in latter periods to this second variable (i.e. the fact that there is no feedback from the second to the first) is not a sufficient condition to declare a distinct causality, but it is a necessary condition.

The causality test which Sims describes involves regressing the dependent variable on lagged, current and leading values of the independent variable (using historical data). If the lengths of lags and leads used are sufficient, an F test for the significance of the lead coefficients as a group should reveal whether there is any feedback effect between variables (i.e. whether causality is bi-directional).

The data used in Sims' study to test the directions of causality between money and income were quarterly from 1947:1-1968:IV and included the monetary base (currency + adjusted reserves), M_1 (currency + demand deposits) and both nominal and real gross national product. Sims filtered the natural log of all the variables because he said "it is important that the assumption of serially uncorrelated residuals be approximately accurate [p. 545]." The filtering equation is

$$(1 - 1.5*\text{lag} + .5625*\text{lag}_2)*\text{Variable}. \qquad (2.1)$$

The variables of GNP and money were regressed on one another in combinations using both leads and lags. Six different models, including different measures of money and varying lag lengths, were tested. The GNP figure in his first set of regressions was nominal GNP and monetary aggregates were the base and M_1 money stock. "The F-tests shown are for the null hypothesis that all right-hand side variables except trend and seasonal dummies had zero coefficients [p. 546]." The F-statistics were significant for the models in which GNP was regressed on only lags of a money variable (suggesting that money "causes" GNP). When the lead values of the variables were added (which would capture feedback effects from income to money), the F-statistic fell below the level required for significance (at the 10 percent level) in both the model using M_1 and the monetary base. The value of the overall F-statistics for the models in which the money variables were regressed on leading and lagging values of GNP may suggest that money affects income (if the leading coefficients $\neq 0$) or that income has feedback effects on money (if the coefficients on the lagged variables $\neq 0$).

If nominal GNP doesn't have feedback effects on money, then in the regression of GNP on the monetary base (MB) and M_1, small insignificant coefficients should be generated for leading money values. Only one out of the four coefficients for leading MB values was significant (at the 10 percent level) in the GNP regression on the MB, and the F-statistic for the null hypothesis that the joint coefficients on the four leading values were zero was only 0.39 (which fails to allow rejection of the null). For the GNP on M_1 regressions, none of the coefficients for the four leading values were significant and the F-value that they were jointly and significantly different from zero was 0.36. Conversely, the regression of M_1 on GNP produced two significant coefficients on leading values of the independent variable (again out of four), and the F-statistic for the null hypothesis that the joint coefficients on leading values of M_1 were zero was 4.29 (which is significant at the 5 percent level). The monetary base on nominal GNP regression had three of the four coefficients on the leading values of the explanatory variable come up significant, and the F for the joint significance of all four leading coefficients was 5.89 (which allows the null to be rejected).

In Sims' own words "these results allow firm rejection of the hypothesis that money is purely passive, responding to GNP without influencing it. They are consistent with the hypothesis that GNP is purely passive, responding to M according to a stable distributed lag but not influencing M [p. 547]." Finally, Sims ran the above regressions for real GNP with the monetary base only. Although the monetary base was not as significant in explaining real GNP as it was in explaining nominal GNP, Sims notes the "values of coefficients and F-statistics were much the same with (real) GNP as dependent variable as with (nominal) GNP the dependent variable. Future lags were again highly significant for MB on GNP regressions and highly insignificant for the reversed relation [p. 548]."

QUESTIONS ON THE IMPORTANCE OF MONEY AND INTEREST RATES

The research reviewed above supported a causal role of money relative to national economic cyclical fluctuations. This section reviews some more recent research which assigns a lesser role for money relative to cycles. Some of the conclusions are reached by authors who had originally reached monetarist conclusions (e.g. Sims and Weiss). It was essentially a change in econometric techniques which changed the conclusions of these researchers. That is why it is important to study a leading series under these techniques. The second reason for this section is to highlight the use of VARs and their previous application to cyclical and investment research. A common feature of this research to be reviewed and the previous research discussed is that leading time series aggregates are absent from consideration.

In their book *Lectures on Macroeconomics* (1989), Blanchard and Fischer present correlations between innovations in GNP and other economic variables including money and nominal and real interest rates. The authors describe an innovation as the residual from an autoregressive integrated moving average procedure on the respective variable. They found that innovations in money growth were positively correlated with innovations in GNP at a lead of two quarters and also contemporaneously. Also, they reported that nominal interest rate innovations had a negative correlation with GNP innovations at a lead of one, two, and three quarters but a positive contemporaneous correlation. Real interest rate innovations only had a negative correlation at a lead of two and three quarters and a direct relationship with GNP innovations at both a one quarter lead and contemporaneously. These findings lead Blanchard and Fischer to conclude that ". . .theories that emphasize money shocks have to confront the correlations among interest rates, money, and output [p. 20]" because ". . .if money is the major source of fluctuations in GNP, then its contemporaneous effect on GNP cannot be explained through interest rates [p. 20]."

In their paper "Business Cycles: Real Facts and a Monetary Myth" (1990), Kydland and Prescott attempt to re-test some of the relationships that have generally been thought to exist between certain macro variables (e.g. those of the monetary base and M_1 leading deviations in output from trend). Their results differ from those previously found because they use an unconventional detrending method. This method (described on pages 8 and 9 of their article) minimizes a weighted value of the sum of the squared errors from a non-linear time trend and changes in the growth rate of the trend component. They report only simple correlations between the deviations from trend of other macro variables and deviations from trend in real GNP. The results of interest here involve those between deviations in money aggregates and GNP. They found, using quarterly data from 1954-1989, that not only did deviations from trend in the monetary base not lead GNP deviations but actually lagged GNP deviations. Also, they found that deviations from trend in M_1 were positively correlated with deviations from trend in GNP but only contemporaneously. Of the money aggregates tested, only deviations from trend in M_2 could be shown positively to lead deviations from trend in GNP over the years considered. The lack of support they find for the monetary base or M_1 leading the cycle leads the authors to reject the hypothesis that monetary policy has had any influence on the business cycle and that the leading M_2 significance shows that "credit arrangements" have been more important.

In a paper entitled "Money, Credit, and Interest Rates on the Business Cycle", Benjamin Friedman (1986) uses different statistical techniques to approach the cyclical relationships between GNP and various financial variables using annual data from 1947 to 1982. The first statistical technique used was simple correlations. Correlation coefficients were reported for the growth rate of real GNP to the growth rates of current and one-year lags of nominal M_1, the nominal yield on commercial paper and the nominal yield on Baa rated corporate bonds. Friedman found the coefficients between GNP and M_1 to be small and insignificant. The correlation coefficients, however, between GNP and both of the interest rates were negative (ranging from -.34 to -.65) and significant.

The second statistical technique employed was a bivariate autoregressive procedure. Here again, relationships were estimated between the growth rates of nominal M_1 and the long and short term rates. It was found here that money and both interest rates were significantly "causally" prior to GNP and were all exogenous to reciprocal effects from GNP. Only F-statistics were presented for this procedure.

Five-variable vector autoregressions (which included growth rates in real GNP, nominal M_1, outstanding credit, the GNP deflator and the return on commercial paper) were the most complex statistics used by Friedman. Again, though, his data were annual. He estimated for two sub-samples - 1947-1965 and 1966-1982. Money was the only financial variable to be strongly significantly prior to GNP in the years 1947-1965. The short term interest rate was the only financial variable to be significantly prior to GNP in the 1966-1982 sub-sample. Friedman notes that when a time trend is added to this five- variable system, the short term interest rate became the only significant explanatory variable for real GNP in either sub-sample (it removes the importance of money in the 47-65 sub-sample).

Friedman concludes by saying that many of the economic fluctuations in the post-war era seem to be tied in some way to money and interest rates. He continues, however, by saying that the estimations of the actual relationships are not very robust and do not support a theory of stable and systematic causality from money or interest rates to real economic activity.

The first part of this section has reported on findings which have used simple statistical techniques or limited data series to refute the view that money and/or interest rates either lead or "cause" GNP deviations from trend. The latter part of the section reports on research which, using more depth, carries this approach further to show that money doesn't affect other real variables (such as real interest rates) and that interest rates per se don't affect real macro time series (specifically GNP and business fixed investment).

In his article "Comparison of Interwar and Postwar Business Cycles: Monetarism Reconsidered" (1980b), Sims presents statistical evidence which refutes the findings of his 1972 article and provides a brief theoretical explanation of the new findings. His statistical interpretations were of vector autoregressions (VARs) using monthly data for the periods 1920-41 (interwar) and 1948-78 (postwar). The variables in his first set of VARs were the money stock (M_1), industrial production and the wholesale price index. Each VAR consisted of 12 lags of each of the variables (converted to natural logs) with no trend term. From these, Sims reports on the percent of the variation in the innovations in each variable that is explained by itself and the other variables at a 48 month forecast horizon.

The results for M_1 from this first set of VARs were that it explained 92 and 97 percent of the variance in its own innovations in the inter- and postwar periods respectively. The variance in the innovations of industrial production was explained 28 and 44 percent by its own lags in the inter- and postwar periods and 66 and 37 percent by lags of M_1 over the same periods. The wholesale price index accounted for 6 and 18 percent of the variance in the innovations of industrial production in the inter- and postwar periods. These results support the "priority" of money and show that, while it may affect production, it is exogenous to a reciprocal effect.

However, Sims finds that, when a short term nominal interest rate is added to the VAR system, money's importance in explaining industrial production and its apparent exogeneity are both reduced, specifically in the postwar period. The percent of postwar innovation variance in industrial production attributable to money declines to 4 percent in the four-variable VARs. The percent of variance in the innovations of industrial production explained by nominal interest rates in the postwar period, however, was 30 percent. Also of importance was the fact that past money, after the inclusion of the nominal rate, could explain only 42 percent of the postwar innovation variance of its future values. Nominal interest rates accounted for 56 percent of the M_1 variance in innovations in the postwar period. Sims' conclusion from this is that "some of the observed comovements of industrial production and money stock are attributed to common responses to surprise changes in the interest rate [p. 253]."

The possible theoretical explanation Sims gives for the relationship he uncovered was, by his definition, Keynesian in nature. He begins by commenting that for this theory to work, instantaneous capital adjustments must be costly to the firm and so they begin adjustments to the stock of their capital prior to the change actually being needed. Given this, he says that if it is believed by businesses that the marginal product of capital will decline in the future, they will begin now to adjust their capital stock by decreasing their rate of investment. If this decline in investment leads the price of capital goods to fall, then the interest rate will increase at least until the expected decline in capital's marginal productivity becomes a reality. This component of the theory explains why past increases in interest rates would do well in explaining present and future declines in production. The combination of increasing interest rates and an expected decline in production would then cause money demand to drop. If money supply is changed month to month as a direct response to money demand, this would explain why money is no longer "prior" or exogenous in this theory when interest rates are included. Also it explains why, without the inclusion of interest rates, money would seem to "cause" production (because its changes lead changes in production) and why this apparent causality is removed by the interest rate (because its changes lead or "cause" the changes in money).

Sims' work, and the conclusions drawn from it, may suffer from having examined an inappropriate output measure. The problem from using industrial production in an examination such as this is may be that it moves coincidentally over the cycle with overall GNP. If the true nature of the economy's behavior is for interest rates to affect a certain category of variables which move, on average, before aggregate production and which in turn affect aggregate production, omitting the "leading" variables from consideration could alter or even reverse the statistical implications of the relationships that exist between money, interest rates and the economy. The possible business cycle chain that is of concern here would differ from Sims' in the following way. RI, which generally makes its cyclical turns prior to the turns in the cycles of national product measures, would be sensitive to the rate of interest. With, for example, declining interest rates (brought on by real factors in the economy such as falling output, changing expectations, money, etc), RI would begin to increase. The increase in RI spending would act as an impulse to increase both money demand and then GNP. This outline of causation, running from interest rates through RI into GNP, explains the same facts as Sims' theory above and still allows a causal role for interest rates. Further, this chain of causation possibly can allow for a causal role for money. If a decline in interest rates is engineered through an open-market purchase of securities by the Federal Reserve, the resulting increase in the money supply will be exogenous and then will cause interest rates to fall. As a consequence, RI will rise and will lead aggregate output.

In their article "Money, Real Interest Rates, and Output" (1985), Litterman and Weiss begin by emphasizing that, in a number of currently held macro theories, real interest rates are the vehicle through which money can affect the real output of the economy. Their claim is that money does not affect the expected real interest rate (and that in fact the real rate is exogenous) and therefore that this linkage cannot be correct. By real rate exogeneity, Litterman and Weiss (L&W) mean that expected (ex ante) real rates are "Granger-Causally prior, relative to a universe containing money, prices, nominal rates and output [p. 130]." That is, the real interest rate "...is governed only by its own past history, with no separate influence coming from...[p. 154]" the aforementioned variables.

L&W attempt to recalculate the results of Sims (1972). To do this they ran both a three- and four-variable VAR. The three variable VAR included four lags of the industrial production index (their output proxy), the M_1 money stock and inflation. The four variable VAR included these three plus a short term nominal interest rate (quarterly average on 90-day T-bills). Data were quarterly from 1949:2-1983:2. A Granger causality test was performed which strongly rejected "the exogeneity of output with respect to money [p. 131]" in the three-variable VAR. Although output was still not exogenous relative to money, money's importance did decline when the nominal interest rate was added to make the four-variable VAR. It is the authors' final conclusion that nominal rates add predictive power for output to the estimated equation because they partly anticipate future inflation.

Of course, it could be the case that nominal rates hold output predicting power because of the information that they embody about real rates. Fama (1982) presents a study that would disagree with this last proposition (as Litterman and Weiss make note). In order to test whether it is the expected real component of short term nominal rates that affect output, L&W begin by defining the expected real rate, r_t, as

$$r_t = R_t - t\Pi^{t+1}, \tag{2.2}$$

where R_t is the nominal interest rate on 90 day T-bills and $t\Pi^{t+1}$ is the time t forecast of time $t+1$'s inflation rate (i.e. a one quarter ahead inflation forecast). The inflation expectation used in calculating the unobservable real rate of interest is rational and follows the form

$$t\Pi^{t+1} = E(\Pi_{t+1} \mid Y_{t-k}, M_{t-k}, R_{t-k}, \Pi_{t-k}; k=0,1,2,3) \tag{2.3}$$

where

Y = Industrial Production Index,
M = M_1 money stock and
Π = Inflation calculated from changes in CPI - shelter.

The authors forecast the inflation rate over the period in question and develop a series of the ex ante real rate which is then tested for exogeneity (i.e. tested as to whether or not it explains its own future behavior and whether the coefficients on other lagged independent variables are zero). The null hypothesis of real rate exogeneity could not be rejected.

Having determined that the calculated series of their definition of the expectation of the real rate is exogenous, Litterman and Weiss examine how they believe this would affect the role money would (or could) play in three macro models using the real rate of interest as the transmission mechanism. The three models are the Keynesian IS-LM, Lucas-Barro and Grossman-Weiss models.

Having accepted that the expected real rate is exogenous, the authors list three "auxiliary hypotheses" under which money could still affect real output in a typically defined Keynesian IS-LM model.

1. That "it was the deliberate objective of Fed policy to set expected real rates in such a way that" they "followed a univariate autoregressive process [p. 135]."
2. "That the IS curve is horizontal [p. 135]."

3. "That over the sample period, most variations in money supply were passive responses to money demand shocks [pp. 135-36]."

They note that while the third possibility is not easily dismissed, "the data's failure to reject the hypothesis of real rate exogeneity casts strong doubt on the Keynesian notion that monetary policy has affected output changes through the real rate of interest [p. 136]."

By Lucas-Barro models Litterman and Weiss are referring to the new-classical, incomplete information models that depend on unperceived changes in money to distort the perceived terms of trade. They note that while these models appear to be consistent with the finding of real rate exogeneity, appending them "to be consistent with the fact that there are substantial serial correlations in most macroeconomic time series [p. 136]" would substantially change this result. L&W say that "theories which emphasize a confusion between unperceived monetary injections and persistent real factors affecting the ex ante real rate would generally predict a systematic response of the real rate to changes in real production [p. 136]." If this were the case, these types of theories would be incompatible with the finding of an exogenous real rate.

The Grossman-Weiss model also relies on insufficient information but here in the area of the discount rate between consumption in adjoining periods. They say the model determines the ex ante real rate as $r_t = (1-\alpha)[C_{t+1}-C_t]$ where C is the log of per capita consumption and α the coefficient of risk aversion. Litterman and Weiss state that an exogenous real rate here is compatible "if and only if per capita consumption is exogenous relative to the same universe [p. 137]." Again, though, they comment that if the model is appended to encompass serially correlated consumption and productivity shocks, then real rates, as defined above, would no longer be exogenous and, thus, this theory also would be incompatible with their findings.

A final finding of interest from the article was a report on the decomposition of variance for the innovations in nominal interest rates. Litterman and Weiss find that innovations in real interest rates and innovations in expected inflation comprise approximately equal parts of the innovations in nominal interest rates (44 percent of the variance being explained by expected inflation and 56 percent by real interest rates). Given this, they look to see whether the predictive power of nominal rates over their output variable (industrial production) can be equally divided into the predictive power of each of its two components. For industrial production, it was found that nominal rates provided the best explanation, closely followed by expected inflation innovations with almost no variance explanation coming from real interest rates. That is, "expected inflation innovations are a sufficient statistic for predicting real variables [p. 155]" and that real rates play no causal role.

Lawrence and Siow (1985) use a system of VARs to test the interest and output sensitivity of real business producer equipment (BPE) spending (quarterly from 1947-1980). They also test to see whether nominal interest rates are better predictors of BPE spending than are real rates due to their power to anticipate or predict future GNP. They use VARs because they dislike the rigid structural partial equilibrium investment models which have been used to study various forms of business fixed investment in the past. They note that varying (and opposing) results are generated from such structural models and say the blame must be at least in part due to the structure of these models (e.g. deciding only by theory which variables affect investment and which of those should be exogenous in the model).

The authors believe that it is "an open question" whether short or long term rates should be used in such a study. In following Hall (1977), they believe that short term rates would be "relevant when there is no cost of adjustment mechanism and there is free entry into the industry [p. 360]." They test the usefulness of long versus short term rates for explaining BPE spending by running basic OLS regressions which included lagged values of these interest rate variables. They reject the null hypothesis that the joint coefficients on the lagged values of the short term interest rate were zero at the 5 percent significance level. The null hypothesis that the joint coefficients on the lagged long term interest rate were equal to zero, however, could not be rejected even at the 10 percent level of significance. Given this they use the three-month T-bill discount as their interest rate variable.

In the article, Lawrence and Siow present a causality test showing that the short term nominal interest rate "causes" real output and is therefore a predictor of real output, making it "necessary to separate the predictive effect of nominal rates on investment versus the discounting effects [p. 367]."

Their VARs included equations which had lagged values of BPE spending, real rates and real output and others which had lagged values of BPE spending, nominal rates, inflation and either actual real output or anticipated real output. They say empirically that short term real rates have only a "small effect on postwar quarterly product equipment spending [p. 362]." They continue to say that

> Short term nominal rates, on the other hand, have a profound and persistent effect on measured investment, due to the fact nominal rates are forward looking with predictive power in explaining future anticipated GNP. Once we control for anticipated GNP, the impact of nominal rates-in terms of magnitude and persistence-is significantly damped [p. 362].

The final conclusions are that their statistics support an accelerator type investment theory because an equation which did not include the real interest rate but did include lagged values of anticipated GNP could sufficiently explain BPE spending. They note that "we can thus infer from our statistical tests that real rates are of a second order of magnitude relative to forecasts of GNP in predicting investment [pp. 371-72]."

This section has examined the branch of recent research which has begun to empirically reduce the role attributed to money and the interest rate transmission of money with respect to macro cyclical fluctuations. Specifically, the last two articles have introduced systems of VARs (those including expected inflation, real interest rates and anticipated output) which have helped in reducing money's role and will therefore be a main element of the research proposed here. However, these last two VAR investigations reviewed have dealt with a series that lags the general business cycle and one that coincides with the general business cycle, while in this book a series that leads the general business cycle will be examined.

WORK ON RESIDENTIAL INVESTMENT AND HOUSING

This section reviews existing research on RI. It reports on the current empirical knowledge of RI related to interest rates, income and inflation.

In an article entitled "Monetary Policy Influence on the Economy - An Empirical Analysis", Akhtar and Harris (1987) use a structural regression model which they describe as "based on a fairly standard framework [p. 19]" to test the interest elasticities of real residential construction spending and to test for a change in this elasticity after the banking sector of the economy began to be deregulated. They used quarterly data from 1960-1986. They say that while "the short-to medium-term monetary policy influence seems to be quite uncertain and difficult to estimate [p. 20]" longer run effects of interest rates on residential construction spending have "been substantial and significant [p. 19]."

Their real residential construction spending equation is

$$HOUSE = b_0 + b_1 INCOME + b_2 INTER + b_3 CHUN + b_4 DUM$$
$$+ b_5 HOUSE(-1). \qquad (2.4)$$

Here the variables are in logs and are defined as follows:

INCOME $=$ Real disposable personal income averaged over 8 quarters ("a measure of permanent income"),

CHUN $=$ The change in unemployment from the preceding period,

DUM $=$ 1 when deposits at savings and loans declined,

HOUSE(-1) $=$ A one quarter lag of real residential construction spending,

INTER $=$ A weighted average of cost of capital values for owner occupied and rental housing with the cost of capital variables taking the general form

$$(p^h/p)[d + i(1-t) - p^h]Tax \qquad (2.5)$$

and the variables here are defined as:

p^h/p $=$ Price of housing relative to a general consumer price index,

d $=$ Rate of capital depreciation,

i $=$ Nominal interest rate on fixed mortgages,

p^h $=$ Distributed lag on past housing inflation,

t $=$ Marginal income tax rate,

Tax $=$ Variable to capture other tax effects.

The short run interest elasticity of residential construction spending figured from this model was -0.2 (with a t value of 4.4), and the long run interest elasticity was calculated to be -0.81. The long run income elasticity of residential construction spending was also slightly less than unity. The long run elasticities here were derived by dividing the coefficient on the respective variable by one minus the coefficient on the lagged dependent variable. This is possible due to the variables being in log form.

The style of this article is representative of the vast majority of empirical work which has investigated RI. While its findings are of importance, a different technique was used for this book (that introduced by Sims [1980a]) which seems more suited for this type of macro investigation and lends more credibility to the results.

In an article entitled "Real and Nominal Interest Rates and the Demand for Housing", Schwab (1983) empirically examines whether nominal rates in themselves are the crucial factor in housing demand functions or one of its components (real rates or expected inflation). Schwab mentions that strict neo-classical theory has housing demand specified as only a function of real rates (as far as discount or cost of funds variables are concerned). He continues, however, that expected inflation or nominal rates might have roles to play in the real world. Expected inflation may come in to play by causing a temporary cash flow problem, and some have said that the nature of a mortgage commitment (a long term contractual commitment based on a nominal loan amount and nominal interest rate) suggests that the nominal rate alone should be used to specify housing demand functions. Schwab says that if housing demand would be properly specified as a function of the nominal rate "that changes in either expected inflation or the real rate would have the same effect on demand [p. 181]."

Schwab's data came from a study of 8700 families in the Philadelphia suburbs from 1968.4-1975.3 who purchased FHA insured homes. The partial equilibrium demand function he estimated took the form

$$Z = \alpha_0 + \alpha_1\rho + \alpha_2\pi + \alpha_3Y + \alpha_4P + \alpha_5OMR + \alpha_6FS + \epsilon$$

$$(2.6)$$

Where:

Z   = Stock of purchased housing,
ρ = Long term real interest rate,
π = Long term expected inflation,
Y   = FHA effective income (their measure of permanent income),
P   = Relative price of housing,
OMR = FHA estimate of expenses on operating, maintenance, repairs and taxes and
FS = Family size.

"The time series for π is a weighted average of current and past actual inflation [p. 184]."

Schwab tests for the importance of ρ, π and nominal rates under the following three conditions:

i) "if $\alpha_2 = 0$ then only the real interest rate determines the demand for housing [p. 187]."

ii) "if $\alpha_1 = \alpha_2$ then the nominal interest rate is the appropriate variable in a housing demand equation and it is unnecessary to distinguish between its two components [p. 187]."

iii) If α_1 and α_2 are significantly different from one another while both are significantly different from zero, then both real rates and expected inflation are important but for separate reasons and nominal rates have no role.

His results for the income and price elasticities were that the former was positive and the latter was negative while both were slightly less than unity. His examination of the three conditions revealed that the coefficients on the calculated values of expected inflation and the real rate were both negative and significant. At the same time, the t statistic for $\alpha_2 - \alpha_1 = 0$ allowed for a strong rejection of the null of equality. Schwab's final conclusion was that housing demand is a function of expected inflation and the real rate but that the nominal rate would not be a necessary or appropriate independent variable in such an equation.

Other articles have looked at the two components of the nominal rate and how they relate to housing. These articles are not discussed in depth here because they used cross sectional data or did not use a housing stock, construction or residential investment dependent variable. Their results are mentioned, though, because they are related to the topic at hand.

Kearl (1979), Boehm and McKenzie (1981) and Follain (1982) found a negative relationship between expected inflation and housing demand or construction. Hendershott (1980) found that the demand for single family housing was directly related to the expectation of a higher future rate of inflation. Finally, Van Order and Dougherty (1991) say that anticipated inflation did not matter in the high inflation decade from 1970 - 1979 but that only real rates held predictive power (although they admit a down payment constraint is binding for some households).

Since the removal of ceilings on interest rates began in the early 1970's and particularly since the passage of the Depository Institutions Deregulation and Monetary Control Act (DIDMCA) in 1980, economists have been concerned with a possible change in the interest sensitivity of certain sectors of the economy. Among these sectors is housing or residential investment because it has generally been considered to be one of the more interest sensitive components of GNP. This section looks at three articles which, using various measures of housing investment and interest rates (including different term lengths), attempt statistically to determine whether there has been a change in the response (presumed a priori to be a decline) of housing or residential investment to the rate of interest. The three articles are "The Changing Interest Sensitivity of the U.S. Economy" by Kahn, "Do Interest Rates Still Affect Housing?" by Pozdena, and an article which has already been partially discussed above, "Monetary Policy Influence On The Economy - An Empirical Analysis" by Akhtar and Harris. Each article begins by stating that the main reason for the expected decline in the interest sensitivity of this sector is due to the elimination of disintermediation-led credit rationings which were due primarily to financial regulations. In the post DIDMCA era, funds do not have to be removed from savings and loans (S&L's) when interest rates in other markets are high because S&L's, through financial deregulation, are now allowed to compete for funds by using interest rates. Before DIDMCA, however, S&L's, which were until the 1980's the main source of mortgage funds, had their deposits decline and therefore their loaning ability cut when their regulated maximum rate of interest fell too far below other rates in high interest rate episodes. This lack of supply of funds exacerbated any housing demand interest sensitivity, making the overall decline in residential construction more pronounced in these high rate periods. Another reason given in two of the articles for the expected decline in housing investment's interest sensitivity is the growth of the secondary mortgage market. The sale of bonds off a group of approved mortgages in these markets provides a national source of funds to borrowers with a competitive return to potential lenders.

The structure of the model and definition of the variables for residential construction spending in the Akhtar and Harris paper were outlined above (pp. 23-24). The conclusion was that residential investment was interest sensitive and more so than either producer durable equipment spending or consumer durable purchases (these last two variables were included in their article but were not reported on above). Its long run interest elasticity was slightly below one. The same model as above was used to test for the possible change in the interest elasticity of residential investment over time. Their pre- and post-deregulation sub-samples were the years 1960-74 and 1975-86. They chose 1974 as the critical year because they said after 1973 the interest ceiling on large negotiable CD's was removed and that deregulation was continuous from then through the early 1980's. The results were that the long run interest elasticity did decline in the later period, but only slightly, from -0.928 to -0.872. A dummy variable to capture periods of credit rationing (when deposits at S&L's declined) confirms the suspicion that credit crunches did serve to reduce this type of spending more in the earlier period than now. One possible explanation they give for the small decline in the interest elasticity overall, even though the credit rationing contribution declined substantially, was that

> with an unprecedented rise in the 1970's, interest rates may have reached a threshold where they start to have a stronger effect on spending. It may be that financing costs are an important influence on profits and investment decisions only at high rates [p. 20].

Kahn (1989) uses a form of a vector autoregression in his examination of RI's interest sensitivity. The VARs included real residential investment spending and the nominal federal funds rate (because the author said it was most responsive to money policy). His pre-deregulation period was 1955:4-1979:3 and his post-deregulation period 1983:1-1989:2. He comments that the reason the period 1980-

1982 was omitted was because it "reduces the likelihood that structural causes for changes in the economy's interest sensitivity might be mistaken for the effect of a change in monetary policy regime [p. 23]," as the Fed was not targeting the federal funds rate during that time.

From the estimated equation, the author makes predictions of how RI would react to a permanent one percentage point increase in the federal funds rate. His results were that "before 1980, this interest rate change caused residential investment to fall about $7 billion after six quarters. Today, . . . , the effect is down to about $2 billion [p. 24]." Thus, he concludes RI is now less responsive to both money policy and the rate of interest.

Pozdena also uses a series of VARs to test whether the interest sensitivity of the housing sector has changed. He also investigates the possibility that interruptions in the net flow of funds into S&L's had, prior to DIDMCA, caused a larger response in the housing sector than they currently would. His data were monthly and his pre- and post-deregulation periods were 1960-1982 and 1983-1989, respectively. He used the break at 1982 instead of 1980 (when DIDMCA was actually passed) because he says all the regulations which could possibly have caused interest rates to affect housing from the supply side (through credit rationing) weren't completely phased out until after 1982. Variables which were included in the VARs were 1) the number of housing starts (STARTS), 2) the 90-day nominal T-bill rate (TBILL), 3) the difference between long and short term nominal rates (LNGMSHRT), used to capture changes in expected long term inflation or the effect of a shifting yield curve, and 4) net changes in share balances and deposits at S&L's (FUNDTOT).

In a VAR including only lagged values of T-bills and housing starts and another including those two variables and the variable LNGMSHRT, a Chow test for differing parameters suggests that in both cases the model's coefficients could not be considered identical between the two sub-samples at the 90 percent confidence level. In the simplest VAR (STARTS and TBILLS only), a variance decomposition measured at 24 months showed that the rate on T-bills explained 60.4 percent of housing start variation prior to 1983 and only 21.5 percent after 1982. From the tables in his paper it is easy to see that the interest rate is less important in explaining housing starts after deregulation was fully phased in.

A second VAR included the variables STARTS, TBILLS and FUNDTOT. As above, the values are the percent of the variance of housing starts explained, measured at 24 months. Again, the results serve to illustrate the declining importance of interest rates on the housing sector after 1982. It suggests, however, contrary to the theory hypothesized in this and the previous two articles, that the net fund flows into S&L's is more important after deregulation than before.

The impulse response of housing starts to a permanent one standard deviation increase in the interest rate (for the second VAR), in the pre 1983 sub-sample, predicts that housing starts would decline by more than 70,000 units (at 9 and 12 months) and would remain below their initial level for more than 24 months. For the post-1982 sub-sample, however, the same increase in the interest rate on T-bills would cause less than a 40,000 unit decline (reaching its lowest level at five months) from the initial level and cause housing starts to remain below the initial level for only 16 months. The predicted response of housing starts to a one   standard deviation increase in the net flow of funds into S&L's, pre 1983, was an increase of over 20,000 units above the initial level for at least 24 months. After 1982, however, the same increase in net fund flows never causes an increase above the initial level as high as 20,000 units in housing starts, and housing starts are above their initial level for only 10 out of the 24 months plotted.

Pozdena concludes, because both the variance decompositions and impulse responses lead to the same conclusion, that the interest rate does not affect housing after 1982 to the extent that it did in 1982 and before. Although the variance decompositions and impulse responses gave differing results for the fund flows analysis, Pozdena concludes that changes in the variable are not as important after 1983 and that this is one contributing factor to the decline in housing's interest sensitivity.

Both Kahn and Pozdena admit that limitations of their models are that there is little data from the post deregulation period, and that the economy has not suffered either a downturn in overall economic activity or a sharp upturn in interest rates in their post deregulation periods. There may also be other drawbacks to their work. First, there was a radically changing inflation environment over the course of the 1980's. Also, both Kahn and Pozdena use short term interest rates. Throughout the 1980's, short and long term rates did not always move together, and the differences between their behaviors were not consistent. Work incorporating these facts into a VAR model could significantly change their results.

III

Methodology

This chapter begins with a section providing an explanation of VARs. The explanation begins with a presentation of the statistical underpinnings which leads into a presentation of the strengths and weaknesses of the technique as expounded in the macroeconometric literature. The final section lists the variables used in the analysis of chapters 4 and 5 along with sources from which the data were obtained.

VECTOR AUTOREGRESSIONS

The discussion of the methodology and applications of VARs in this Section comes from two groups of work. The first is a group of papers written on the econometric and statistical theory of VARs. This group includes Sims (1980a, 1981), Hakkio and Morris (1984) and Chapter 12.5 from Pindyck and Rubinfeld (1991). The second group consists of articles which primarily have applied VARs but also include a discussion of their general use and estimation. This second group includes Sims (1980b), Gordon and King (1982), Litterman and Weiss (1985), Runkle (1987), Spencer (1989) and Todd (1990). Two comments also considered are McCallum (1983) and Sims (1987). In some cases a specific author is cited directly; otherwise, the discussion will be a summary of a number of these authors at one time.

VARs are atheoretical, non-structural models which require very few theoretical assumptions or restrictions to be placed on the individual regression equations. In VARs, all variables can be

31

considered endogenous and trend components can optionally be included. While VARs include lags of each of the variables under consideration, there is no rigorously defined or maintained lag structure for any equation. Hakkio and Morris (1984) argue ". . . that a VAR is an unrestricted reduced form of an unknown structural model [p. 40]." One is free to use these models for the estimation of relationships or in making forecasts without a specific model having been explicitly drawn out and made, through whatever manipulations, econometrically testable. Each endogenous variable is at the same time considered as both a dependent variable and a regressor. This allows relationships and feedback effects, including those which theory may not have suggested, to play roles where applicable.

Sims (1980a) introduced VARs because he believed there existed a problem with identification of the macro-forecasting models which existed at the time. He argued that the assumptions econometricans used to identify these models were "incredible" and "cannot be taken seriously." Sims claimed that if a variable appeared as an explanatory variable in one equation of a system then it belonged as an explanatory variable in each equation of the system. Whereas estimatable reduced forms of simultaneous equation systems are made up of a few exogenous and lagged endogenous variables from the system (those included having been chosen directly or indirectly by the investigator's explicit theoretical specification), a VAR includes lagged values of each variable in the system in each equation in the system. While this reduces the ability to test any particular theory, it probably enhances the study of the dynamic relationships between variables and the ability to forecast such variables (at least in the short run).

As an example of the form that VARs take, the equations for a system including the variables C and K would be:

$$C_t = \alpha_c + \sum_{i=1}^{n} \beta_{c,c,i} C_{t-i} + \sum_{i=1}^{n} \beta_{c,k,i} K_{t-i} + e_{c,t} \qquad (3.1)$$

$$K_t = \alpha_k + \sum_{i=1}^{n} \beta_{k,c,i} C_{t-i} + \sum_{i=1}^{n} \beta_{k,k,i} K_{t-i} + e_{k,t} \qquad (3.2)$$

The value n is the number of lags imposed on each endogenous variable.

There is a statistic which can be used to aid in the determination of the proper lag length. The method is very similar to an F-test being used to determine whether the reduction in the residual sum of squares of an equation's fit (due to an extra variable having been added or an extra lag being included in the equation) is significant. This standard F-test approach is inapplicable here, though, because any change in lag length will affect the entire system of equations. The statistic to be calculated in the case of VARs is the a-statistic. Its calculation begins with the estimation of systems which are identical except for the lag length imposed. The procedure continues by "comparing the determinants of the restricted and unrestricted covariance matrices of the equation errors. The test statistic a can be computed as

$$a = (T - k)(\log |\Omega^R| - \log |\Omega^U|) \qquad (3.3)$$

where T is the number of observations, k is the number of estimated parameters in each equation, and $|\Omega^R|$ and $|\Omega^U|$ denote, respectively, the determinants of the contemporaneous covariance matrix of the residuals of the restricted and unrestricted models [Gordon and King, 1982 pp. 209-210].[1] The a-statistic is distributed as a χ^2 with $E_n*E_q*(Lg_j - Lg_i)$ degrees of freedom, where E_n is the number of endogenous variables, E_q is the number of estimated equations and Lg the number of lags on the two models being compared (j > i).

Hakkio and Morris (1984) note that it is useful ". . . to write the system of equations as a classical recursive system [p. 11]." This means that current error terms from the equations (called innovations) are allowed to enter other equations in a recursive fashion. The equations in the system are ordered and each equation can only be affected by the contemporaneous innovation from previously ordered equations. The first equation, therefore, would not be affected by any contemporaneous innovations. The second equation would be affected by the innovation from the first and so on.

As an example of this recursive entrance of contemporaneous errors, if the system of equation 3.1 and 3.2 were ordered C, K, then $e_{c,t}$ would enter the equation for K_t. However, $e_{k,t}$ would enter neither equation. If a third equation existed and was ordered after K, both $e_{c,t}$

and $e_{k,t}$ would enter its function. Given a C,K ordering, the equations 3.1 and 3.2 would be rewritten, after consideration of the effect of contemporaneous innovations, as

$$C_t = \alpha_c + \sum_{i=1}^{n} \beta_{c,c,i} C_{t-i} + \sum_{i=1}^{n} \beta_{c,k,i} K_{t-i} + e_{c,t} \qquad (3.4)$$

$$K_t = \alpha_K + \sum_{i=1}^{n} \beta_{k,c,i} C_{t-i} + \sum_{i=1}^{n} \beta_{k,k,i} K_{t-i} + \theta_{k,c,i} e_{c,t} + e_{k,t} \qquad (3.5)$$

Therefore, if this equation system were collapsed to matrix notation the β matrix would be RxRn in dimension where R is the number of variables and the θ matrix would be a lower triangular matrix of the dimension RxR. Because of the ensuing character of the θ matrix, the sequence of the equations imposed on the system is called a triangularization of the system. As Gordon and King (1982) note, ". . . the assumption about causal ordering of contemporaneous errors in a VAR system amounts to a decision about admitting current variables into the estimating equation [p. 212]."

If the C and K variables were put into a matrix identified as Q, then the last two equations would be written in matrix form as

$$Q_t = \beta(L)Q_t + \theta e_t \qquad (3.6)$$

L in equation (3.6) above is the lag operator.[2] Sims (1981) implies that if the variables making up a matrix such as Q are stationary the matrix notation above can be rewritten as a moving average representation with only the stochastic error terms as right hand side variables. The change from an autoregressive to a moving average process is done by the following transformation (once the β matrix of coefficients is known).

$$Q_t = \beta(L)Q_t + \theta e_t \qquad (3.7)$$

$$Q_t - \beta(L)Q_t = \theta e_t \qquad (3.8)$$

$$Q_t(I - \beta(L)) = \theta e_t \qquad (3.9)$$

$$Q_t = (I - \beta(L))^{-1}\theta e_t \qquad (3.10)$$

As Hakkio and Morris (1984) note, "the ith element of e_t, e_{it}, represents the unanticipated component of the ith element of ...[Q]... at time t [p. 19]." They continue "the coefficient matrix. . . represents the response of the system to a one standard error shock, or innovation, in e_t [p. 19]." This innovation would be a one time temporary shock to the system. That is, the coefficient matrix determines the reaction of the system to an innovation in e_t which is zero both before and after time t. An impulse response function is simply a tracing out of this moving average representation for a particular variable in the system to the innovation of a particular variable (the same or another) in the system. The impulse responses plotted in chapters 4 and 5 will have been calculated in this way. Sims (1980a) explains that these "resulting system responses are fairly smooth, in contrast to the autoregressive lag structures, and tend to be subject to reasonable economic interpretation [p. 21]." That is, even though the coefficients on the lagged independent variables are often difficult to interpret due to a systematic temporal oscillation, the impulse response functions will still allow for reasonable economic conclusions.

Impulse response functions are only one of the methods used to analyze the effects that variables in a VAR system have on one another. The other tool for analyzing such effects are variance decompositions. The purpose of a variance decomposition is to show what percent one variable's innovations explain of the squared forecast error of another variable. The following discussion on the calculation of variance decompositions is a summarization and modification of Hakkio and Morris (1984) pp. 24-26. In making forecasts m periods ahead with the model specified in terms of current and lagged residuals, one would need to know the errors between time t and time t+m. The value of these residuals, of course, are not known at time t and their expected value would be zero. Given this, the error in the forecast would be the actual value of the residuals between time t and time t+m multiplied by their respective coefficients. These coefficients, which will be signified by d, come from the quantity $(I - \beta(L))^{-1}$ in equation (3.10). The squared forecast or prediction error (SFE), for example, of an innovation in C on the variable K at time t+m in summation notation would be

$$SFE = \sum_{i=1}^{m-1} d_{k,c,i}^2 e_{c,t+m-i}^2 + \theta_{k,t+m}^2 e_{c,t+m}^2 \qquad (3.11)$$

for i < m. For values of i greater than or equal to m, the actual residuals would be known at time t. Equation (3.11) breaks down to the square of the proper d and θ coefficients multiplied by the variance of the e_c terms. The value of the e_c^2 terms are known and therefore a number representing the squared forecast error for a time t+m forecast of the response of K to an innovation in C can be calculated. Likewise, the squared forecast error for K at time t+m to an innovation in each of the variables in the system could be calculated as

$$SFE = \sum_{i=1}^{m-1} d_{k,c,i}^2 e_{c,t+m-i}^2 + \sum_{i=1}^{m-1} d_{k,k,i}^2 e_{k,t+m-i}^2 + \theta_{k,t+m}^2 e_{c,t+m}^2 \qquad (3.12)$$

for i < m. Taking (3.11) as a ratio to (3.12) gives the portion of the total forecast error variance for K, in an m step ahead forecast, that is attributable to innovations in C. The variance decompositions in the following two chapters will be calculated in this way.

As in any econometric technique which deals with time series variables, the problem of non-stationarity is important in VARs. For proper estimation, the variables in a VAR system should have a constant mean and variance (i.e. a mean and variance which are not time dependent). A trend component can be included as an exogenous variable for those series known to have a deterministic trend component.

The efficacy of VARs for short term forecasting is highly touted by its proponents and leaves little room for criticism by its opponents. The ability to test theories or to determine the effect variables have on one another from within a VAR, however, is the subject of much criticism. The critics take one of two approaches. The first approach is that VARs are "measurement without theory" due to their atheoretical nature and do not allow for exact measurements or differentiation between competing theories. The second form of criticism centers on the fact that the results obtained from a VAR analysis are not robust (e.g. parameter estimates and variance decompositions are not stable through seemingly mild changes in the model).

With regard to the first criticism, the fact that it is partially true would not preclude using VARs in this analysis. A VAR would not allow the ability to distinguish whether monetary policy affects the economy as monetarist or Keynesians would suggest. This, however, is not the goal. The goal is to see whether money has affected RI over the past four decades and how any apparent relationship between the two changes when interest rates, expected inflation, financial disintermediation or deregulation are considered. VARs are well suited for this purpose. Instead of establishing a new equation for a simultaneous equations system for each new variable that is to be considered, the variable, and its appropriately lagged values, can simply be added into the VAR system and the data allowed to determine what should affect it and what it should affect. While any one specific parameter estimate will not be very accurate, the conclusions reached using a VAR concerning whether money has affected RI and whether the aforementioned considerations change this conclusion (and how much so) should be as precise as could be achieved using other time series techniques. It should be noted, however, that although VARs cannot be designed to test explicitly any particular theory, their results can often lend support to one of two contradictory theories. For example, if this research suggests that money and nominal interest rates lead movements in RI, which in turn acts as an impulse for the cyclical movements of GNP, then it will indirectly lend support to monetarism or Keynesian economics over real business cycle theory.

The second line of criticism also has some validity. Most of those who have criticized VARs on the grounds that they are not robust use the Sims (1980b) article as a base. This article was discussed in chapter 2 pp. 16-18. Authors who have done this include Runkle (1987), Spencer (1989) and Todd (1990). These writers have concentrated on Sims' result showing that money accounted for only 4 percent of the variation in unanticipated movements in industrial production within a variance decomposition at a 48-month forecast horizon. They have made what they consider modest changes in Sims' model and report on how their resulting estimates are different. The biggest difference is that they have found money accounted for a larger portion of the unanticipated fluctuations in industrial production than did Sims (from 4 percent to around 20 or 30 percent). Some of their changes, however, I do not believe were modest or innocuous. These changes include adding a trend as an exogenous variable and changing the specific series used to represent other variables (e.g. representing inflation as changes in the consumer as opposed to the producer price index). Differences such as these would most likely lead to significant changes in the results from any statistical procedure. Valid criticisms which are specific to VARs are that different triangularizations of the system to allow for a re-ordering of the recursive entrance of contemporaneous errors and changes in the lag length of the variables can at times significantly change the results. Given this, it was important in this research before estimation began to try to properly determine the appropriate lag length using the a-statistic and throughout estimation to consider various orderings of the system's variables. If changes such as re-orderings had drastically changed the implied dynamic interactions from the VARs, it would have suggested that VARs are not an appropriate tool for such an analysis. However, since the estimates were robust through numerous changes, this lends a credibility to the results not present in results from a single estimation of a structural equation.

DATA

The data used in this research have been taken from *Business Conditions Digest* (the 'Historical Data for Selected Series' tables), *Survey of Current Business*, and the *Federal Reserve Bulletin*. The series used in chapter 4 are quarterly from the year 1950 until the third quarter of 1990. Those used in chapter 5 are through the first quarter of 1991. All of the data except those for the interest rate variables have been seasonally adjusted at the source. Any variables noted in the list below to be in real (constant dollar) values were deflated at the source. All interest rates (or bond yields) listed below came from the source as nominal values and any conversions to real values are noted and explained in the text.

The following historical series are used:

Real Gross National Product.
Real Gross Private Residential Fixed Investment.
Implicit GNP Deflator.
Federal Funds Rate.
Average Prime Rate charged by banks.
Secondary market yields on FHA mortgages.
Nominal Monetary Base.
Nominal M_1 money stock.

NOTES

1. This test statistic is a modification of the one originally presented in Sims (1980a) [pp. 17-18].

2. The lag operator is common in time series notation. As an example of how it is defined, $L^1 Z_t = Z_{t-1}$. The highest order of the operator in a VAR is the maximum number of lags of the endogenous variables, n. For a full discussion of the lag operator, see Pankratz(1983) chapter 2.

IV

Empirical Results For The Full Sample Period

This chapter reports empirical findings on RI for the entire sample period 1950.1 - 1990.3. Before results are presented, concerns such as lag length and data transformations are discussed. First, taking into account the criticisms of Sims' VARs discussed in the last chapter, it is important to calculate properly the necessary lag length using the a- statistic. Also related to those criticisms, there is the need to determine whether the variables should be transformed due to non-stationarity. Specifically related to this analysis, it is necessary to determine a method for calculating a series for anticipated inflation.

DATA TRANSFORMATIONS

The plotted autocorrelation coefficients (ACC.) in figure 4.1 show that real RI, real GNP, nominal M_1, and the nominal FHA mortgage rate are all non-stationary. Were the variables stationary, the ACCs would have fallen to near zero after a lag of a few quarters. The failure of ACCs to quickly fall to zero implies that there exists a trend in the variable which is making it correlated with itself in adjoining periods through time. A trend rules out the possibility that a variable can have a constant mean through time. And without a constant mean, truly efficient estimation of a variable's parameters in an equation is not possible. Following the procedure of Eichenbaum and Singleton (1986), Runkle (1987), Spencer (1989) and Todd (1990) a time trend will be included as an exogenous variable in the VARs to correct the problem.

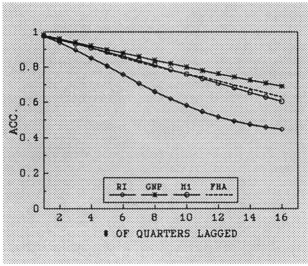

Figure 4.1 Correlograms for RI, GNP, M1 & FHA

INFLATION EXPECTATIONS

A real interest rate is defined as a nominal interest rate minus the level of expected inflation. Expected inflation, however, is not a directly observable series. Therefore, an expected inflation rate must be calculated for each circumstance where it or a real rate is required. Because of the character of the debt instruments associated with RI, the real interest rate needs to be calculated using an inflation forecast that is more comprehensive than simply a one-quarter ahead forecast. That is, since the majority of RI involves long term contractual commitment at an originally stated nominal rate of interest, it will be the general pattern of inflation or persistent shifts in the level of inflation over the term of the commitment that will be important in real rate calculation. Closely following the methods of Hendershott and Schilling (1982) and Van Order and Dougherty (1991), anticipated inflation will be defined as a weighted average of past years' inflation. The weights will be an exponentially decaying constant (.5), and actual inflation values over the past 3 years (12 quarters) will be used. The time t expectation of the level of inflation for time $t+1$ ($tIFL^{t+1}$) will be

$$tIFL^{t+1} = \sum_{i=1}^{12} (.5)^i IFL_{t+1-i} \qquad (4.1)$$

In order for the sum of the weights to equal unity, the values of the weights on quarters 11 and 12 are equal. This calculation of the anticipated level of future inflation has a correlation coefficient of .794 (which is significant at the 1 percent level) with the actual inflation rate at all times $t+1$ over the sample. Inflation seems to be sufficient for predicting its own future value. While the calculated expectation here is long-term and adaptive in nature, the high correlation just mentioned suggests that it should be similar to a short-term rational expectations calculation.

LAG LENGTH DETERMINATION
This section reports the a-statistics computed for the test of the significance of the increasing number of lags of the endogenous variables. Here the three-variable VAR containing M_1, RI, and GNP is used. The checks for improved performance of extra lags were begun after a four-quarter start. A minimum four-quarter lag is used here, following the standard established in previous VAR business cycle research. At least a year's worth of lags is considered necessary if the initial and reciprocal effects between money and the economy are to be established. The failure to use at least a year's worth of lags in systems where money is included would leave this research open to legitimate criticisms and doubts of validity. As reported in the previous chapter, though, some have even suggested that a year's worth of lags may be insufficient to capture all relevant information. This view is not widely held and examinations which have considered lags of one and a half or two years have, *ceteris paribus*, not reached very different conclusions from those using only a one year lag. The a-statistics were computed, therefore, to determine whether additional lags appear to be appropriate. Table 4.1 shows the calculated a-statistics and their corresponding critical values at the 95 percent confidence level. Increases from 4 to 5 lags and from 4 to 6 lags are not statistically significant in improving the explanatory power of the overall system of equations. Given this, a 4-quarter lag will be used in the following VARs.

Table 4.1. a - Statistics For Differing Lag Lengths

INCREASED LAG FROM	a - STAT	CRITICAL a - STAT
4 to 5	3.33	16.92
4 to 6	20.37	28.87

EMPIRICAL RESULTS

Regressions for M1, RI and GNP

To begin the analysis only three variables are included in a VAR: nominal M_1, real RI and real GNP. Two orderings of the system were run, one with M1 first and one with it last, to determine whether the results are robust. When ordered first, M_1 explains about 17 percent of the forecast error variance in RI (from one to 8 quarters). When it is ordered last, however, it explains less than one half of one percent. Within both orderings, M_1 appears to be exogenous to the system (explaining approximately 92 percent of its own variance) and GNP appears to be most heavily affected by RI. Table 4.2 shows the variance decompositions for RI, table 4.3 reports those for GNP and table 4.4 those for M_1.

Table 4.5 contains the correlations among the contemporaneous innovations in the system's variables (i.e. between the VAR's regression residuals at time t). The strongest correlation is that between RI and GNP (.47). The contemporaneous correlation between M_1 and RI, however, is also strong (.38). The contemporaneous link between M_1 and GNP is weak in the figures shown here.

Figure 4.2 and 4.3 plot the impulse response functions for RI to one sample period standard deviation shocks in the system's variables for each of the orderings. The impulse responses visually show how money's effect on RI is drastically reduced when it is re-ordered from the beginning to the end of the causal chain of contemporaneous errors. Its effect is dropped from causing a five billion dollar increase in RI at six quarters to causing less than a half billion dollar increase at six quarters. The effect of GNP on RI is robust across the re-ordering of the system's equations, but the effect is small and negative over the entire 8 quarters. This negative effect would not be surprising, though,

Table 4.2 Variance Decomposition of RI For The System of M1, RI and GNP

TRIANGULARIZATION	FORECAST HORIZON	PCT. OF FORECAST ERROR VARIANCE EXPLAINED BY		
		M1	RI	GNP
M1, RI, GNP	2 quarters	16.7	83.2	0.1
	4 quarters	17.5	80.6	1.9
	6 quarters	16.6	78.9	4.5
	8 quarters	15.7	76.6	7.7
RI, GNP, M1	2 quarters	0.2	99.7	0.1
	4 quarters	0.2	97.9	1.9
	6 quarters	0.1	95.3	4.6
	8 quarters	0.2	92.1	7.7

Table 4.3 Variance Decomposition of GNP For The System of M1, RI and GNP

TRIANGULARIZATION	FORECAST HORIZON	PCT. OF FORECAST ERROR VARIANCE EXPLAINED BY		
		M1	RI	GNP
M1, RI, GNP	2 quarters	2.9	36.6	60.5
	4 quarters	7.2	44.1	48.7
	6 quarters	11.2	48.1	40.7
	8 quarters	14.7	49.9	35.4
RI, GNP, M1	2 quarters	0.1	39.0	60.9
	4 quarters	0.4	51.0	48.6
	6 quarters	1.1	58.5	40.4
	8 quarters	2.0	63.2	34.8

Table 4.4 Variance Decomposition of M1 For The System of M1, RI and GNP

TRIANGULARIZATION	FORECAST HORIZON	PCT. OF FORECAST ERROR VARIANCE EXPLAINED BY		
		M1	RI	GNP
M1, RI, GNP	2 quarters	98.3	0.5	1.2
	4 quarters	96.7	1.2	2.1
	6 quarters	96.1	1.6	2.3
	8 quarters	95.5	2.3	2.2
RI, GNP, M1	2 quarters	86.6	10.5	2.9
	4 quarters	87.6	7.9	4.5
	6 quarters	88.3	6.9	4.8
	8 quarters	89.4	5.8	4.8

Table 4.5 Correlations of Contemporaneous Innovations For The System of M1, RI and GNP

VARIABLES	M1	RI	GNP
M1	1.00	.	.
RI	0.38	1.00	.
GNP	0.12	0.47	1.00

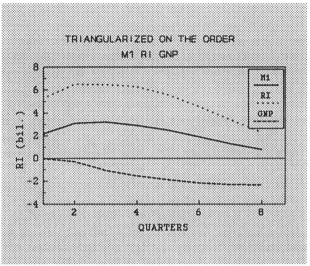

Figure 4.2 Impulse Response of RI to Innovations
in M1, RI and GNP

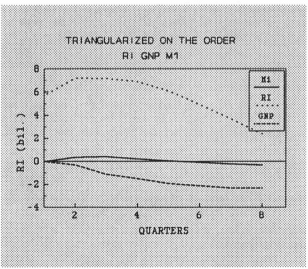

Figure 4.3 Impulse Response of RI to Shocks in
M1, RI and GNP

if RI is found to be sensitive to interest rates and a rising GNP, through increasing money demand, raises the rate of interest. However, the positive effect of RI on GNP is stronger than that of GNP on itself.

The most immediate conclusion from the statistics above is that RI has a heavy positive influence on GNP determination and that no reciprocal relation exists. The priorness found, of course, does not guarantee causality. In this case though, there is a strong theoretical justification for the assumption of causality. First, RI is a part of GNP. Further, any expenditure on residential investment is subject to a multiplier which can act to increase real GNP. The initial conclusions regarding money are that, if it directly affects RI, it does so very quickly and for only a short period of time. In addition, if money affects GNP directly, it does so only after a lengthy lag and is subjected to a minimal feedback effect. Table 4.5 reports a strong correlation for RI and M_1 contemporaneously and the first ordering in table 4.2 shows that the direct effect of M_1 on RI is stronger in the earlier forecast horizons. Table 4.2 and figures 4.2 and 4.3 show that when contemporaneous considerations of M_1 are removed from estimation (by re-orderings) that money no longer has a direct effect on RI. Therefore, if any effect of money upon RI does exist, it occurs at time t and fades quickly. The relationship between M_1 and GNP is not very strong or systematic. The only place any effect is revealed is in the first ordering of table 4.3. In this case M_1 begins to play a role in determining GNP only after a year's time, and the role becomes increasingly large after a year and a half and two years.

VARs with the inclusion of the nominal FHA mortgage rate

Three different triangularizations are estimated for the system which included the previous three variables plus the nominal FHA mortgage rate. These three orderings are i) M_1, FHA, RI, GNP; ii) RI, FHA, M_1, GNP; and iii) M_1, RI, GNP, FHA. Table 4.6 reports the variance decompositions for RI and table 4.7 those for GNP. The FHA rate reduces the apparent exogeneity of money. Over all orderings and forecast horizons, the FHA rate accounts for an average of 16 percent of the forecast error variance of nominal M_1. This result is similar to that of Sims (1980b). As for the FHA rate itself, even in the system where it is ordered last, it accounts, on average, for 90 percent of its own variance over all forecast horizons. GNP and M_1 account for about five percent of the variance in FHA in that ordering. The effects of all

Table 4.6 Variance Decomposition of RI For The System Including a Nominal Interest Rate

| TRIANGULARIZATION | FORECAST HORIZON | M1 | PCT. OF FORECAST ERROR VARIANCE EXPLAINED BY | | |
			FHA	RI	GNP
M1, FHA, RI, GNP	2 quarters	7.6	3.7	88.6	0.1
	4 quarters	4.7	24.2	70.8	0.3
	6 quarters	3.2	38.9	57.0	0.9
	8 quarters	3.6	45.3	49.3	1.8
RI, FHA, M1, GNP	2 quarters	0.0	4.3	95.7	0.0
	4 quarters	0.2	25.6	73.9	0.3
	6 quarters	1.2	40.6	57.3	0.9
	8 quarters	2.7	47.0	48.5	1.8
M1, RI, GNP, FHA	2 quarters	7.6	4.3	88.1	0.0
	4 quarters	4.7	25.0	69.4	0.9
	6 quarters	3.2	39.2	55.5	2.1
	8 quarters	3.6	44.9	44.8	3.7

Table 4.7 Variance Decomposition of GNP For The System Including a Nominal Interest Rate

TRIANGULARIZATION	FORECAST HORIZON	PCT. OF FORECAST ERROR VARIANCE EXPLAINED BY			
		M1	FHA	RI	GNP
M1, FHA, RI, GNP	2 quarters	2.7	0.7	32.0	64.6
	4 quarters	4.8	2.3	33.0	59.1
	6 quarters	5.8	9.9	30.7	53.6
	8 quarters	5.5	19.7	27.4	47.4
RI, FHA, M1, GNP	2 quarters	0.2	0.5	34.8	64.5
	4 quarters	0.4	2.5	37.2	59.9
	6 quarters	0.8	10.3	35.3	53.6
	8 quarters	0.9	20.2	31.5	47.4
M1, RI, GNP, FHA	2 quarters	2.6	0.0	32.2	65.2
	4 quarters	4.8	3.9	32.8	58.5
	6 quarters	5.8	13.2	30.3	50.7
	8 quarters	5.6	23.9	26.8	43.7

the system's variables on both RI and GNP are remarkably robust through the various orderings and re-orderings of the causal chain of contemporaneous errors.

The FHA rate and RI appear about equally important in the determination of the latter over the longer forecast horizons. Innovations in money seem to play a small role in the system's overall effect on RI and again only contemporaneously. Innovations in both RI and GNP account for a substantial portion of the forecast error variance of GNP. Although GNP is the most important (explaining about 56 percent of its own variance on average), it is in no way exogenous to the effects of RI (which accounts for approximately 32 percent of the GNP variance). The FHA rate and M_1 account for 9 and 3 percent of the forecast error variance of GNP, respectively. The variance decompositions for FHA are shown in table 4.8 and those for M_1 are printed in table 4.9. Of considerable importance is the robustness of results (with the exception of the effects of M_1) across the three orderings.

The strongest contemporaneous correlation, as shown in table 4.10, is again between RI and GNP (.48). The only other correlations of any significant size are between M_1 and RI and GNP (.29 and .15, respectively). Of importance in this system is the positive and small correlation between M_1 and the nominal FHA rate (.02). Whether the correct theory is that Federal Reserve increases (decreases) in money causes a decrease (increase) in the rate of interest, or that increases (decreases) in interest rates lower (raise) the money stock endogenously through lowering (raising) money demand (as Sims suggested), the time t correlation between M_1 and FHA should be negative. The most obvious explanation for this anomaly is that FHA is a long term rate and it and money may not react quickly to one another.

Figures 4.4, 4.5 and 4.6 trace the impulse response functions of RI to shocks in the system's variables for each of the orderings. As a comparison indicates, the impulse responses of RI to itself, GNP and FHA are very robust across re-orderings of the variables. Although the changes that GNP cause to future RI are relatively small, they are again negative in this system, as was found in the three-variable system. The magnitude of the effects of innovations in RI and FHA on RI are similar in this system. A shock in RI causes almost a six billion dollar increase in itself at two quarters and has a positive effect on itself over all 8 quarters. FHA shocks reduce RI by almost six billion dollars at five or six quarters and have a negative effect on RI for all 8 quarters.

Table 4.8 Variance Decomposition of FHA For The System Including a Nominal Interest Rate

TRIANGULARIZATION	FORECAST HORIZON	PCT. OF FORECAST ERROR VARIANCE EXPLAINED BY			
		M1	FHA	RI	GNP
M1, FHA, RI, GNP	2 quarters	0.4	98.6	0.4	0.6
	4 quarters	2.8	95.2	0.2	1.8
	6 quarters	5.7	91.7	0.3	2.3
	8 quarters	7.9	88.4	0.6	3.1
RI, FHA, M1, GNP	2 quarters	0.1	98.5	0.9	0.5
	4 quarters	2.0	95.3	1.0	1.7
	6 quarters	4.1	91.8	1.8	2.3
	8 quarters	5.6	88.5	2.8	3.1
M1, RI, GNP, FHA	2 quarters	0.4	96.5	0.6	2.5
	4 quarters	2.8	92.2	0.4	4.6
	6 quarters	5.7	88.4	0.6	5.3
	8 quarters	7.9	84.8	0.9	6.4

Table 4.9 Variance Decomposition of M1 For The System Including a Nominal Interest Rate

| TRIANGULARIZATION | FORECAST HORIZON | M1 | PCT. OF FORECAST ERROR VARIANCE EXPLAINED BY | | |
			FHA	RI	GNP
M1, FHA, RI, GNP	2 quarters	92.6	6.3	0.6	0.5
	4 quarters	81.7	17.2	0.5	0.6
	6 quarters	77.3	22.1	0.3	0.3
	8 quarters	77.4	22.0	0.3	0.3
RI, FHA, M1, GNP	2 quarters	88.6	5.9	5.0	0.5
	4 quarters	79.2	16.4	3.8	0.6
	6 quarters	73.8	21.2	4.6	0.4
	8 quarters	72.3	21.2	6.3	0.2
M1, RI, GNP, FHA	2 quarters	92.6	5.9	0.6	0.9
	4 quarters	81.7	16.4	0.6	1.3
	6 quarters	77.3	21.4	0.4	0.9
	8 quarters	77.4	21.6	0.4	0.6

Table 4.10 Correlations of Contemporaneous Innovations For The System With a Nominal Interest Rate

VARIABLES	M1	FHA	RI	GNP
M1	1.00	.	.	.
FHA	0.02	1.00	.	.
RI	0.29	0.03	1.00	.
GNP	0.15	0.09	0.48	1.00

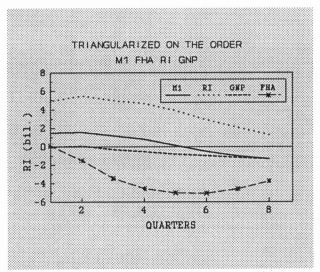

Figure 4.4 Impulse Response of RI to Innovations
in M1, FHA, RI and GNP

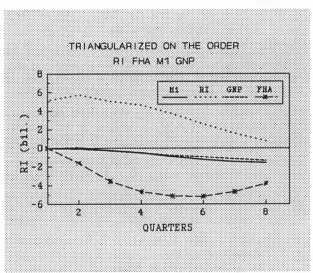

Figure 4.5 Impulse Response of RI to Shocks in
M1, FHA, RI and GNP

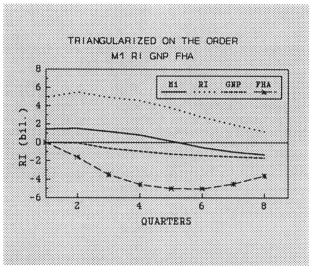

Figure 4.6   Impulse Response of RI to Unanticipated
Changes in M1, FHA, RI and GNP

VAR system with a real interest rate

The next group of regressions discussed here included a calculation of the real FHA mortgage rate (RFHA) in place of the nominal rate used in the last sub-section. A real rate is of interest here for two related reasons. First, much of neo-classical theory would suggest that the real rate is relevant in all investment decisions and would provide a stronger statistical link between mortgage rates and RI. If the link between RFHA and RI, however, is not stronger than that between FHA and RI these results combined with the results from the VARs containing expected inflation (which will follow in this chapter) should help to determine whether either of its components gives the nominal rate the explanatory power over RI found in the last sub-section or whether the nominal rate is important in itself.

Table 4.11 shows the variance decomposition of RI. The real rate calculation has smaller effects on the system than did the nominal rate (from table 4.6). Regardless of the ordering, RFHA fails to account for more than 3.5 percent of the forecast error variance of either RI or GNP. Because of the lack of strong effects, results are reported here

Table 4.11 Variance Decomposition of RI For The System With a Real Interest Rate

TRIANGULARIZATION	FORECAST HORIZON	PCT. OF FORECAST ERROR VARIANCE EXPLAINED BY			
		M1	RFHA	RI	GNP
M1,RFHA, RI, GNP	2 quarters	15.9	1.3	82.6	0.2
	4 quarters	15.0	3.3	79.0	2.7
	6 quarters	13.2	3.4	76.6	6.8
	8 quarters	12.0	3.4	73.8	10.8

for only one ordering and only for RI. Although money has an effect
on RI from the ordering shown in table 4.11, its effect falls to around
one percent when subjected to re-orderings (i.e. when its
contemporaneous effects are not considered). When RFHA is ordered
last, it accounts for approximately 2.1 percent of the forecast error
variance in RI.

The innovation correlations, shown in table 4.12, are very similar
to those shown earlier for the variables M_1, RI and GNP. A negative
correlation was found between M_1 and the real interest rate, but it was
very small, -.01.

Figure 4.7 plots the impulse response functions of RI to shocks
in the system's variables under the same ordering as that in table 4.11.
The real interest rate has an immediate negative effect on RI which
lasts over all 8 quarters, but the effect is small (especially relative to
that of the nominal interest rate). The plots of the response to RI and
GNP look very much like those of the previous figures in this chapter.

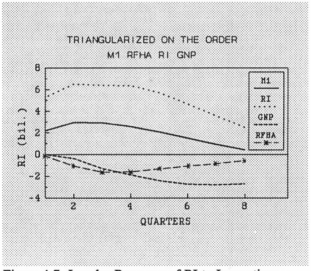

Figure 4.7   Impulse Response of RI to Innovations
in M1, RFHA, RI and GNP

Table 4.12 Correlations of Contemporaneous Innovations For The System With a Real Interest Rate

VARIABLES	M1	RFHA	RI	GNP
M1	1.00	.	.	.
RFHA	-0.01	1.00	.	.
RI	0.38	-0.03	1.00	.
GNP	0.10	0.01	0.48	1.00

Tests of cash flow and Fama-Litterman-Weiss hypotheses

Chapter 2 discussed two reasons why the inflation expectations component of a nominal interest rate may be at least as important as the interest rate itself for determining or predicting future changes in aggregate output variables.

One hypothesis, originally formulated by Fama (1982) and empirically tested within VARs by Litterman and Weiss (1985) and Lawrence and Siow (1985), states that interest rates per se (real or nominal) are of no importance. The important factor, they believe, is the anticipated inflation embodied in nominal interest rates. This anticipation of future inflation is formulated partly on expectations concerning future changes in real output. Fama (1982) begins his hypothesis by developing a quantity theory money demand function which has anticipated changes in output as a right hand side variable in the equation. He also makes the assumption that the imbalance between actual real money balances and the demand for real money balances (due to changes in real output) is corrected through changes in inflation and not by changes in the nominal money stock. Therefore, if economic agents expected real output to increase (decrease) they will expect a concomitant decrease (increase) in inflation. An important conclusion from Fama's work is that expectations about future changes in real activity are tacit in the anticipated inflation rates incorporated into nominal interest rates. Along these lines, Litterman and Weiss note that anticipated inflation in time t is 'significantly and negatively correlated' with output at times t+i.

The second reason previously discussed presents a firm theoretical reason why expected inflation might play a deterministic role for RI, at least. At a constant real rate, an increase in a nominal long-term interest rate reflects anticipated increases in future nominal output or income variables above those dictated by their real changes. These anticipated nominal increases, however, are over long horizons (better measured in years than in months or quarters). Therefore, significant increases in the cost of funds based on increases in future nominal income can cause the funds to be too costly until the income increases are actually realized. Although this has been tested in standard regressions, the approach has usually only involved testing real versus nominal rates.

An ideal procedure for testing the importance of expected inflation (and the magnitude of its importance relative to nominal and real rates) is the VAR. Comparing the size and persistence of the impulse response functions and variance decompositions of RI to various combinations and orderings of these components should shed light on which of them is the most important and the extent of their importance. If the real rate is of little importance in RI but expected inflation is important, VARs with expected inflation and the nominal FHA rate should remove much of the heretofore assigned importance of the FHA rate. If both real FHA and expected inflation are important or if the nominal value of the FHA rate is important in itself, FHA should still be a stronger variable for RI determination (and more robust in its estimation) than either of its two components considered separately. Of course, if expected inflation turns out to be the dominant explanatory variable, it will be difficult to determine whether this is support for the Fama-Litterman-Weiss or cash flow hypotheses.

Two different orderings of a system containing both the calculation of expected inflation (EINF) and the nominal rate (FHA) are estimated along with a system that had only the expected inflation calculation and other system variables but no interest rate. In both orderings which included EINF and FHA, the latter proved to cause larger responses of RI to unanticipated shocks and explained a greater portion of RI's forecast error variance. The results for EINF and FHA, both in terms of absolute numbers and relative to one another, were robust through the re-ordering, with EINF accounting for an average of just under 3 percent of the variance through all forecast horizons and FHA for just under 25 percent. Table 4.13 gives more detail on the results of the variance decomposition for RI and table 4.14 on the same type results for GNP. For GNP, expected inflation becomes increasingly important over longer forecast horizons but it still is overshadowed by GNP itself, RI and FHA.

Again, the correlations among the contemporaneous innovations for this system are very similar to those for the other systems reported above for the variables M_1, RI and GNP. EINF has a small negative correlation with both RI and GNP (-.04 and -.01, respectively). The correlation of the contemporaneous residuals of M_1 and EINF is also small and negative, -.02. All of the correlations among the system's variables are reported in table 4.15. Tables 4.13 and 4.15 suggest that the effect of EINF on RI is more immediate relative to the effect of FHA on RI but weaker and less persistent.

Because the impulse responses of RI to the two orderings of this system were practically identical, only those for the first ordering are

Table 4.13 Variance Decomposition of RI For The System of M1, EINF, FHA, RI and GNP

TRIANGULARIZATION	FORECAST HORIZON	PCT. OF FORECAST ERROR VARIANCE EXPLAINED BY				
		M1	EINF	FHA	RI	GNP
M1, EINF, FHA, RI, GNP	2 qrts	7.1	0.3	3.2	89.3	0.1
	4 qrts	3.8	2.5	22.1	71.2	0.4
	6 qrts	3.1	4.7	34.4	56.4	1.4
	8 qrts	4.7	5.9	39.6	47.5	2.3
RI, GNP, M1, EINF, FHA	2 qrts	0.1	0.1	3.9	95.9	0.0
	4 qrts	0.8	1.8	22.7	73.3	1.4
	6 qrts	3.1	3.7	34.5	55.2	3.5
	8 qrts	5.8	4.9	38.6	45.6	5.1

Table 4.14 Variance Decomposition of GNP For The System of M1, EINF, FHA, RI and GNP

TRIANGULARIZATION	FORECAST HORIZON	PCT. OF FORECAST ERROR VARIANCE EXPLAINED BY				
		M1	EINF	FHA	RI	GNP
M1, EINF, FHA, RI, GNP	2 qrts	2.3	0.1	1.7	39.0	56.9
	4 qrts	3.5	0.3	1.5	43.3	51.4
	6 qrts	3.4	1.9	7.6	41.5	45.6
	8 qrts	2.8	4.9	17.3	36.0	39.0
RI, GNP, M1, EINF, FHA	2 qrts	0.1	0.1	0.1	41.4	58.3
	4 qrts	0.1	0.2	2.0	46.8	50.9
	6 qrts	0.1	1.8	9.8	44.8	43.5
	8 qrts	0.3	4.8	20.2	38.4	36.3

Table 4.15 Correlations of Contemporaneous Innovations For The System of M1, EINF, FHA, RI and GNP

VARIABLES	M1	FHA	EINF	RI	GNP
M1	1.00	.	.	.	.
FHA	0.06	1.00	.	.	.
EINF	-0.02	0.02	1.00	.	.
RI	0.29	0.04	-0.04	1.00	.
GNP	0.14	0.12	-0.01	0.52	1.00

shown here. These are depicted in figure 4.8. Much like the effect of RFHA, the future changes that EINF cause on RI are immediately negative and persistent (8 quarters) but small (never causing more than a two billion dollar decrease). The response of RI to itself is consistent with that from previous systems. It increases its own future value by about six billion at two quarters and has a positive effect over all 8 quarters. The nominal FHA's effect is also consistent with earlier responses. It decreases future RI by five billion dollars at 6 quarters and has a negative effect over all 8 quarters plotted.

To get a second estimation on how strongly EINF affects RI, it was included in a system without an interest rate. Although its importance increased (to just under 7 percent of RI's variance explained, on average, from under 3 percent), it did not approach the importance that has been assigned to it by other investigators relative to GNP, IP, or BFI. The variance decomposition of RI for this system is printed in table 4.16 and the correlations among contemporaneous innovations in table 4.17. In this system, the correlations between EINF innovations and those of M_1 and RI are again negative. Money also appears to have its contemporaneous and short lived effect on RI in this system. Also similar to the other systems above, the largest contemporaneous correlation here is between RI and GNP.

The impulse responses of RI for this system are plotted in figure 4.9. The decrease in RI caused by the shock in EINF is larger in figure 4.9 than in figure 4.8 and almost as persistent. In the system with no interest rate, EINF causes a decline in RI of almost three billion dollars at five quarters and has a negative effect for all 8 quarters. In regressions without EINF (figures 4.4, 4.5 and 4.6), the nominal FHA rate alone causes RI to decrease by twice as much in a shorter period of time and has a negative effect for as long a period of time. Given these numbers, it appears that FHA has substantial predictive power outside its inflation component.

VAR examinations with the monetary base
The monetary base (currency held by the non-bank public + adjusted total reserves of depository institutions) is now considered as an alternative measure of the money stock and monetary policy. Its use should capture whether initial monetary policy in the form of currency injections and reserve increases play an important role in RI determination. Because RI is a leading series, it may be affected directly or indirectly by monetary policy before substantial movements

Table 4.16 Variance Decomposition of RI For The System Including Expected Inflation

TRIANGULARIZATION	FORECAST HORIZON	PCT. OF FORECAST ERROR VARIANCE EXPLAINED BY			
		M1	EINF	RI	GNP
M1, EINF, RI, GNP	2 quarters	13.4	1.6	84.8	0.2
	4 quarters	12.2	5.7	78.7	3.4
	6 quarters	10.3	9.0	73.8	6.9
	8 quarters	9.2	11.0	70.0	9.8

Table 4.17 Correlations of Contemporaneous Innovations For The System Including Expected Inflation

VARIABLES	M1	EINF	RI	GNP
M1	1.00	.	.	.
EINF	-0.08	1.00	.	.
RI	0.35	-0.12	1.00	.
GNP	0.08	0.01	0.48	1.00

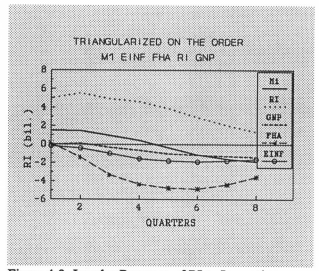

Figure 4.8 Impulse Response of RI to Innovations
in M1, EINF, FHA, RI and GNP

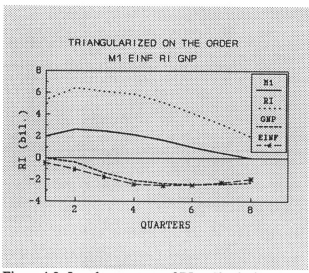

Figure 4.9 Impulse response of RI to Shocks in
M1, EINF, RI and GNP

appear in M_1. This would be the case if a large portion of the cyclical movements in M_1 have been endogenous changes in demand deposits which are responding to real overall economic activity. The monetary base is included in two different systems. The statistical results for these systems are reported in this sub-section.

The first system contains only the monetary base (MB), RI, and GNP. Because of the lack of strong results, only one ordering of this system is examined. RI appears exogenous in this system, explaining 94 percent of its own forecasted error variance on average. The complete variance decomposition for RI is shown in table 4.18. GNP and MB account for just over 3 percent and just under 3 percent of the forecasted error variance in RI, respectively. M_1 appears to be more relevant to RI determination than MB, given these statistical results. In the variance decomposition of GNP, RI accounts, on average, for over 48 percent of the forecasted error variance explanation (see table 4.19). Over the longer forecast horizons, RI is the most important variable in the system regarding GNP determination. The monetary base appears strongly exogenous in this three variable system (in which it is ordered first), explaining over 98 percent of its own forecasted error variance; see table 4.20.

The correlations among the contemporaneous innovations in MB with those for RI and GNP are lower than those for M_1 with RI and GNP (that were reported in table 4.5). Likewise, the effect of a shock in MB on RI over time is less than half of that which was caused by M_1 as shown in figure 4.2. The correlations among this system's time t residuals are printed in table 4.21 and the impulse responses of RI are traced in figure 4.10.

The second system that includes the monetary base also includes the nominal FHA rate. Two orderings of the variables are considered; variance decompositions of RI are shown in table 4.22 for this system. In one ordering, FHA precedes RI and both are preceded by MB, and in the other ordering FHA comes after RI. Regardless of the position of FHA in the causal chain of errors, its explanation of the forecast error variance of RI is both substantial and robust. GNP and MB are insignificant in explaining RI, with neither explaining more than one percent, on average, over both orderings and all forecast horizons. As for the variance in GNP's forecast error, it provides the majority of its own explanation (see table 4.23). Through both orderings and over all forecast horizons, RI accounts for approximately one-third of GNP's variance. The monetary base is insignificant as far as the explanation

Table 4.18 Variance Decomposition of RI For The System of MB, RI and GNP

TRIANGULARIZATION	FORECAST HORIZON	PCT. OF FORECAST ERROR VARIANCE EXPLAINED BY		
		MB	RI	GNP
MB,RI, GNP	2 quarters	2.8	97.1	0.1
	4 quarters	2.5	95.8	1.7
	6 quarters	2.9	93.0	4.1
	8 quarters	2.9	90.1	7.0

Table 4.19 Variance Decomposition of GNP For The System of MB, RI and GNP

TRIANGULARIZATION	FORECAST HORIZON	PCT. OF FORECAST ERROR VARIANCE EXPLAINED BY		
		MB	RI	GNP
MB,RI, GNP	2 quarters	2.3	35.6	62.1
	4 quarters	2.8	47.4	49.8
	6 quarters	4.7	54.0	41.3
	8 quarters	6.1	58.1	35.8

Table 4.20 Variance Decomposition of MB For The System of MB, RI and GNP

TRIANGULARIZATION	FORECAST HORIZON	PCT. OF FORECAST ERROR VARIANCE EXPLAINED BY		
		MB	RI	GNP
MB,RI, GNP	2 quarters	99.7	0.2	0.1
	4 quarters	98.9	0.5	0.6
	6 quarters	98.5	0.9	0.6
	8 quarters	98.0	1.4	0.6

Table 4.21 Correlations of Contemporaneous Innovations For The System of MB, RI and GNP

VARIABLES	MB	RI	GNP
MB	1.00	.	.
RI	0.13	1.00	.
GNP	0.07	0.46	1.00

Table 4.22 Variance Decomposition of RI For The System of MB, FHA, RI and GNP

TRIANGULARIZATION	FORECAST HORIZON	PCT. OF FORECAST ERROR VARIANCE EXPLAINED BY			
		MB	FHA	RI	GNP
MB, FHA, RI, GNP	2 quarters	0.2	2.8	96.9	0.1
	4 quarters	0.4	23.6	75.9	0.1
	6 quarters	0.3	40.9	58.3	0.5
	8 quarters	0.3	51.2	47.6	0.9
RI, GNP, MB, FHA	2 quarters	0.0	3.9	96.1	0.0
	4 quarters	0.5	25.8	72.9	0.8
	6 quarters	0.4	42.6	55.0	2.0
	8 quarters	0.3	51.9	44.7	3.1

Table 4.23 Variance Decomposition of GNP For The System of MB, FHA, RI and GNP

TRIANGULARIZATION	FORECAST HORIZON	PCT. OF FORECAST ERROR VARIANCE EXPLAINED BY			
		MB	FHA	RI	GNP
MB, FHA, RI, GNP	2 quarters	1.9	1.8	31.6	64.7
	4 quarters	1.8	2.0	35.0	61.2
	6 quarters	2.5	8.6	33.6	55.3
	8 quarters	2.9	19.9	29.2	48.0
RI, GNP, MB, FHA	2 quarters	0.4	0.1	32.8	66.7
	4 quarters	0.4	3.3	35.5	60.8
	6 quarters	0.9	12.4	33.5	53.2
	8 quarters	1.3	24.9	28.7	45.1

of GNP is concerned and the FHA rate displays significant explanatory values only after a 6 quarter forecast horizon. The FHA rate appears exogenous in this system (regardless of ordering), explaining over 95 percent of its own forecast error variance, on average, over all forecast horizons. These variance decompositions for FHA are shown in table 4.24. Although MB explains over 90 percent of its own forecast error variance, the conclusion of its strict exogeneity (reached from table 4.20) is partially reversed over the longer forecast horizons by FHA. The complete variance decompositions of MB are shown in table 4.25.

The innovation correlations are printed in table 4.26. The correlations of MB with RI and GNP are both small, and the correlations of FHA with RI and GNP are both positive. The correlation between MB and FHA, however, is negative (-.07). The strongest cross correlation is between RI and GNP (.46).

In both orderings of the system's variables, the impulse response of RI to unanticipated sample standard deviation shocks in RI and FHA

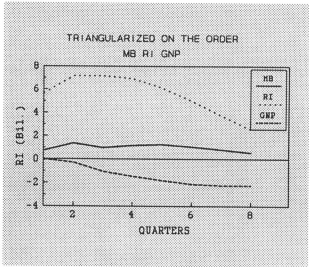

Figure 4.10   Impulse Response of RI to Innovations
in MB, RI and GNP

Table 4.24 Variance Decomposition of FHA For The System of MB, FHA, RI and GNP

TRIANGULARIZATION	FORECAST HORIZON	PCT. OF FORECAST ERROR VARIANCE EXPLAINED BY			
		MB	FHA	RI	GNP
MB, FHA, RI, GNP	2 quarters	0.6	98.7	0.4	0.3
	4 quarters	0.9	97.4	0.7	1.0
	6 quarters	0.6	97.0	1.5	0.9
	8 quarters	0.5	96.3	2.3	0.9
RI, GNP, MB, FHA	2 quarters	0.5	95.9	1.1	2.5
	4 quarters	0.6	93.9	1.5	4.0
	6 quarters	0.4	93.0	2.6	4.0
	8 quarters	0.3	92.0	3.7	4.0

Table 4.25 Variance Decomposition of MB For The System of MB, FHA, RI and GNP

TRIANGULARIZATION	FORECAST HORIZON	PCT. OF FORECAST ERROR VARIANCE EXPLAINED BY			
		MB	FHA	RI	GNP
MB, FHA, RI, GNP	2 quarters	98.2	1.7	0.1	0.0
	4 quarters	90.9	8.7	0.4	0.0
	6 quarters	87.9	11.1	0.9	0.1
	8 quarters	86.0	12.2	1.6	0.2
RI, GNP, MB, FHA	2 quarters	97.4	1.8	0.4	0.4
	4 quarters	90.4	8.7	0.7	0.2
	6 quarters	87.1	11.3	1.3	0.3
	8 quarters	84.7	12.6	2.2	0.5

Table 4.26 Correlations of Contemporaneous Innovations For The System of MB, FHA, RI and GNP

VARIABLES	MB	FHA	RI	GNP
MB	1.00	.	.	.
FHA	-0.07	1.00	.	.
RI	0.04	0.04	1.00	.
GNP	0.08	0.11	0.46	1.00

are almost identical with the responses shown earlier in the book from systems which included the nominal interest rate variable (figures 4.4, 4.5 and 4.6). RI causes nearly a six billion dollar increase in itself at two quarters and has a positive effect over all 8 quarters plotted. An unanticipated shock in FHA causes RI to decrease by more than five billion dollars at five or six quarters and has a negative effect on RI for the entire 8 quarters shown. The impulse responses of RI in this system for the different orderings are traced in figures 4.11 and 4.12.

FURTHER CONSIDERATIONS OF MONEY
AND INTEREST RATES

This section attempts to explain empirically the anomalous results obtained thus far concerning the relationship between money and the FHA interest rate. Surprisingly, the relationship has been found to be positive and very small in magnitude. Two reasons previously have been presented as to why this relationship may have been found. The first reason given was that the FHA is a long term interest rate and the second reason is the nature of the VAR approach. A third possible reason is the use of quarterly data. For examining the variable of interest here (RI), quarterly measurements were the shortest observation interval available. As stated in chapter 3, for the main purposes of this analysis, the VAR is the best procedure. The combination of quarterly data and the lagged structure of the VAR, however, is not ideal for investigating any possible link between money and interest rates. Because a short term rate such as the federal funds rate (FED) should be more sensitive to monetary policy, one- and two-lag VARs using FED in place of FHA were estimated. Again, though, results show correlations which were small and positive.

If there is a direct, contemporaneous effect of monetary policy on interest rates, it must be virtually instantaneous and very short lived (no more than a quarter). Standard regressions were therefore estimated using time t values of the variables involved. The time period for the observations was 1960.1-1990.3. The natural logarithm of the two interest rates (FED and FHA) were regressed individually on the natural log of M_1, GNP and a lag of the rate variable. The estimated money elasticity of the federal funds rate was -1.27 and was significant at the one percent level. The money elasticity of the FHA rate, however, was -0.33 and was not significant at even the 10 percent level. The results are not meant to support one specific direction of

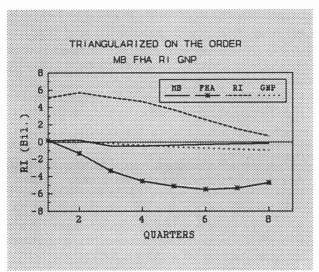

Figure 4.11 Impulse Response of RI to Innovations
in MB, FHA, RI and GNP

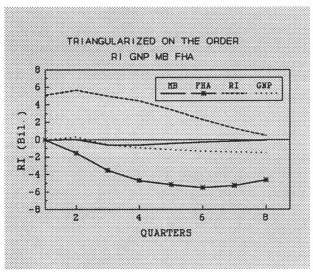

Figure 4.12 Impulse Response of RI to Shocks in
MB, FHA, RI and GNP

causality, but only to show that a negative contemporaneous relationship exists. The results do, however, support the view that the long term rate is less responsive overall to money. While both elasticities were negative, only the money elasticity of the FED was greater than unity.

It is possible that the FHA rate does respond systematically to monetary policy but only when changes in the money stock are above some threshold level. To examine this possibility, correlations were first run on detrended M_1 (DTM1), detrended RI (DTRI) and detrended FHA (DTFHA). The correlation coefficient between DTM1 and DTRI was .181 and that between DTM1 and DTFHA equaled -.221. Correlations also were calculated for a second set of observations that included only periods when the value of DTM1 was at least one-half of one standard deviation, plus or minus, from its mean. For this set of observations, both correlations were larger. The contemporaneous correlation coefficient between DTM1 and DTRI was .424 and that between DTM1 and DTFHA equaled -.366.

While the VARs including FHA from this chapter show a one-way priorness from FHA to M_1, the sign (and magnitude) of the results run counter to what theory would suggest (e.g. that suggested by Sims [1980b]). The results in this section show that the hypothesized negative relationship between money and interest rates can be shown to exist, but they do not lend support to either direction of causality in the form of demonstrated statistical priorness. Therefore, the questions regarding the exogeneity and/or causality of money and interest rates still remain open. Future researchers in this area should be skeptical of the use of VARs and should consider the use of data observation intervals no longer than a month.

SUMMARY

The results in this chapter have established the priorness of FHA to RI and that of RI to GNP. These strong empirical results combined with firm theoretical foundations lend substantial support to the view of causality from FHA to RI to GNP. Of course, these results do not suggest that RI is the only (or main) impulse mechanism for an increasing GNP. Any increase in investment spending, net exports or changes in consumption also will affect the value of GNP. RI is simply the one aggregate that most closely links interest rates to GNP.

It was also found in this chapter that it is the nominal FHA rate that is of primary concern relative to RI. Real rates are of minimal importance (probably because of the nature of a mortgage). Also, while expected inflation may play a role in RI determination by causing a cash flow problem when it reaches high levels, the results of this chapter firmly reject the Fama-Litterman-Weiss hypothesis with regard to RI.

Finally, the regressions reported in this chapter have established that neither RI nor FHA have been highly responsive to each movement in monetary policy over the last 40 years. However, it may be that marked and persistent movements in money have affected both RI and FHA over time. If money has any direct effect on RI (exclusive of its effect through interest rates), it is realized very quickly and the effect is not very strong or long lived.

V

The Effects Of Disintermediation
And Financial Deregulation

The last section in chapter 2 mentioned reasons why RI might have recently become less responsive to interest rates. This chapter begins by expanding on these reasons for possible changing interest sensitivity, follows with a section on variable definition and ends with results of the empirical tests for altered interest sensitivity.

SUPPLY OF FUNDS EFFECTS

The interest sensitivity of an economic aggregate usually refers to the decline (increase) in that type of spending resulting directly from the increasing (decreasing) cost of any borrowed funds necessary to undertake the spending. That is, interest sensitivity usually leads to changes in the amount of requested funds from the borrower's or demand side of the market. For RI, at least, an interest sensitivity may also exist from the other (supply) side of the credit market. As mentioned previously, savings and loans (S&Ls) have been the main supplier of residential mortgage funds through the years. The instruments by which S&Ls accumulated these funds for mortgage lending (i.e., the deposits at the center of the intermediation process) were subject to a regulated maximum rate of interest payable. In periods of high interest rates, depositors at S&Ls have removed their funds in order to seek higher (unregulated) rates of return elsewhere. This disintermediation, or removal of the S&Ls as the financial middlemen, has at times left potential mortgagors without an adequate supply of funds from conventional lenders (regardless of the price they are willing to pay). Of course, RI might also decline in high interest rate episodes directly due to an interest sensitivity from the demand side (i.e. specifically related to the price of the funds). Chapter 4 above helped to establish an interest sensitivity of RI, and this chapter attempts to determine empirically whether this sensitivity stems from the demand or supply side of the credit market or both. Also, because disintermediation credit crunches in the mortgage market have been eliminated by a series of government deregulations, it will be a primary purpose of this chapter to determine whether the post-deregulatory interest sensitivity of RI has declined.

CALCULATION OF A DISINTERMEDIATION VARIABLE

The easiest way to distinguish statistically between the supply side and demand effects of interest rates on RI is to define a variable that coincides with the disintermediation of funds available for mortgages and include this variable separately in the VARs. Because it is the gap between competitive market (short term) rates and the maximum rate payable on savings deposits at S&Ls that leads to the outflow of funds, this gap will be the disintermediation variable in the regressions that follow. Specifically, the gap variable is defined as the difference between the federal funds rate and the regulated maximum interest rate on savings deposits at S&Ls (GAP = Federal Funds Rate - Maximum Rate Payable on Savings Deposits). Negative values of GAP will be set to zero. This is because negative values of GAP (which are associated with periods when S&Ls were allowed to pay depositors more than the federal funds rate) should not increase intermediation through S&Ls and, in any case, would not cause a non-price change in mortgage demand. To try and estimate RI as a function of GAP series that contains negative values would bias the coefficients on GAP towards zero. Of course, the Depository Institutions Deregulation and Monetary Control Act (DIDMCA) passed in 1980 essentially eliminates the gap. Therefore, the GAP variable to be used here becomes more loosely defined after 1980 and is not defined at all after 1982 (the year deregulations regarding S&Ls were fully phased in). Given this, the data set used to examine disintermediation effects will end with the fourth quarter of 1982. After 1982, indirect methods will have to be used to determine if disintermediation played a role prior to the 80's and if the elimination of this regulated effect decreases RI's interest sensitivity in the post DIDMCA era. This will be done by running pre- and post-DIDMCA VARs and comparing RI's interest sensitivity in the two. The pre-DIDMCA VARs use a data set that begins with the first quarter of 1960. This is because it was in the decade of the 60's in which disintermediation could have first begun to play a role in RI determination.

These pre- and post-DIDMCA VARs can also be used to check for a change in RI's money sensitivity. If changes in money caused rates to change and thereby caused disintermediation effects on RI, RI's money sensitivity should decline in the post-DIDMCA era. This will be investigated directly here and has not been examined elsewhere.

EMPIRICAL RESULTS
Direct tests of disintermediation effects

The first system of VARs includes M_1, GAP, FHA, RI and GNP. Two orderings of the variables were considered (one with GAP preceding FHA and vice versa). The variance decompositions of RI for this system are shown in table 5.1. Exclusive of RI itself, M_1 is the most important explanatory variable, explaining almost 20 percent of RI's forecast error variance, on average, over both orderings and all forecast horizons. Following very closely is GAP, which explains just over 19 percent, on average, through all orderings and horizons. Both FHA and GNP explain an average of around 4 percent of RI in this system.

It may appear from the numbers in table 5.1 that RI's historical interest sensitivity has been primarily due to supply side credit crunches. The correlation coefficient of .51 between the time t innovations in GAP and FHA printed in table 5.2, however, suggests that multicollinearity could be confusing the separate effects of the two. Table 5.2 contains the correlations among all the system's variables. Note from the table the strong contemporaneous correlations of M_1 to both RI and GNP.

Figure 5.1 traces out the impulse responses of RI to unanticipated shocks in three of the system's variables. Here also, GAP has a more pronounced effect on RI than does FHA.

In order to overcome possible collinearity problems, GAP and FHA were included separately in VARs that also included M_1, RI and GNP. Two orderings were run in each case. The variance decompositions of RI for the systems including GAP and FHA are in

Table 5.1 Variance Decomposition of RI For The System With Both GAP and FHA, Pre-DIDMCA

TRIANGULARIZATION	FORE-CAST HORIZON	PCT. OF FORECAST ERROR VARIANCE EXPLAINED BY				
		M1	GAP	FHA	RI	GNP
M1 GAP FHA	2 qrts	18.0	5.3	3.7	72.9	0.1
RI GNP	4 qrts	11.5	23.3	2.4	59.1	3.7
	6 qrts	20.0	27.2	2.4	44.5	5.9
	8 qrts	29.4	25.8	1.9	34.7	8.2
M1 FHA GAP	2 qrts	18.0	8.3	0.6	72.9	0.1
RI GNP	4 qrts	11.5	21.9	3.8	59.1	3.7
	6 qrts	20.0	21.3	8.3	44.5	5.9
	8 qrts	29.4	19.6	8.1	34.7	8.2

Table 5.2 Correlations of Contemporaneous Innovations Pre-DIDMCA

VARIABLES	M1	GAP	FHA	RI	GNP
M1	1.00	.	.	.	.
GAP	0.36	1.00	.	.	.
FHA	0.11	0.51	1.00	.	.
RI	0.48	0.27	0.13	1.00	.
GNP	0.49	0.20	0.18	0.51	1.00

Table 5.3 Variance Decomposition of RI For The System Including GAP, Pre-DIDMCA

TRIANGULARIZATION	FORECAST HORIZON	PCT. OF FORECAST ERROR VARIANCE EXPLAINED BY			
		M1	GAP	RI	GNP
M1 GAP RI GNP	2 quarters	19.8	6.9	73.1	0.2
	4 quarters	10.3	28.3	54.2	7.2
	6 quarters	15.3	30.5	39.3	14.9
	8 quarters	21.3	28.2	30.0	20.5
M1 RI GNP GAP	2 quarters	19.8	10.5	68.9	0.8
	4 quarters	10.3	32.6	45.9	11.2
	6 quarters	15.3	32.0	32.4	20.3
	8 quarters	21.3	27.6	25.0	26.1

Table 5.4 Variance Decomposition of RI For The System Including FHA, Pre-DIDMCA

TRIANGULARIZATION	FORECAST HORIZON	PCT. OF FORECAST ERROR VARIANCE EXPLAINED BY			
		M1	FHA	RI	GNP
M1 FHA RI GNP	2 quarters	31.3	2.9	65.4	0.4
	4 quarters	19.1	29.3	49.6	2.0
	6 quarters	12.8	49.8	34.7	2.7
	8 quarters	13.8	54.5	28.1	3.6
M1 RI GNP FHA	2 quarters	31.3	2.3	65.9	0.5
	4 quarters	19.1	26.8	50.8	3.3
	6 quarters	12.8	37.7	35.8	4.7
	8 quarters	13.8	51.1	29.0	6.1

tables 5.3 and 5.4, respectively. Although FHA accounted for a larger
portion of the forecast error variance in RI (29.3 percent) than GAP
(24.5 percent), the difference in the explanatory power of the two was
very small. This again suggests that FHA's historical command over RI
has been primarily (although not exclusively) due to disintermediation
and not demand sensitivity effects.

Tables 5.5 and 5.6 have the correlations among the two system's
innovations. The coefficient between GAP and RI is positive. The
coefficient between FHA and RI, although quite small, is negative.
The contemporaneous correlations between M_1 and RI and GNP are
large in these systems also.

Figure 5.2 has the impulse response of RI for the system
containing GAP and figure 5.3 the same for the system containing
FHA. Here the larger response of RI to FHA is more noticeable. An
unanticipated standard deviation shock in FHA causes RI to decline by
over 6 billion dollars while an identically defined shock in GAP never
causes more than a 3.9 billion dollar decrease.

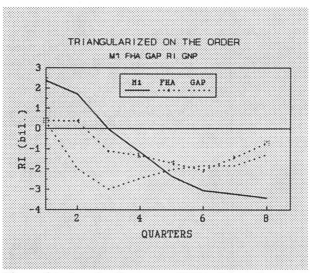

Figure 5.1 Impulse Response of RI to Innovations
in M1, GAP and FHA Pre-DIDMCA

Table 5.5 Correlations of Contemporaneous Innovations For The System With GAP, Pre-DIDMCA

VARIABLES	M1	GAP	RI	GNP
M1	1.00	.	.	.
GAP	0.26	1.00	.	.
RI	0.47	0.25	1.00	.
GNP	0.41	0.26	0.52	1.00

Table 5.6 Correlations of Contemporaneous Innovations For The System With FHA, Pre-DIDMCA

VARIABLES	M1	FHA	RI	GNP
M1	1.00	.	.	.
FHA	0.03	1.00	.	.
RI	0.56	-0.01	1.00	.
GNP	0.48	0.07	0.58	1.00

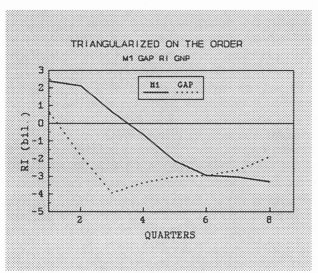

Figure 5.2 Impulse Response of RI to Innovations
in M1 and GAP Pre-DIDMCA

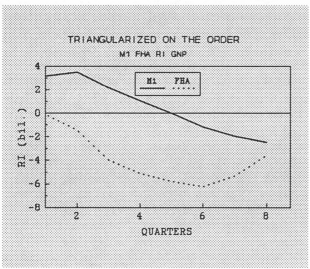

Figure 5.3 Impulse Response of RI to Innovations
in M1 and FHA Pre-DIDMCA

Indirect tests of disintermediation effects

This sub-section presents pre- and post-DIDMCA results. Changes in the response of RI to M_1 or FHA in the post-DIDMCA era will be assumed to be related to the elimination of financial regulations which in the past had significantly contributed to a flow of funds out of S&Ls (and therefore out of the reach of potential home buyers). The data set for the pre-DIDMCA VARs will be 1960.1-1982.4 and that for the post-DIDMCA regressions 1983.1-1991.1.

The first VARs for the split sample included only M_1, RI and GNP (in that order). Tables 5.7 and 5.8 have the results for these VARs in the form of variance decompositions for RI. Two immediate conclusions can be reached from these tables. First, the effect of M_1 post-82 is larger than it was in the pre-83 sub-sample (37.8 percent, on average, compared to 28.7 percent of forecast error variance explained). Second, as was found in chapter 4, the effect of M_1 in the pre-DIDMCA sub-sample is stronger over the earlier forecast horizons and fades over each increasing period while the opposite holds for the post-DIDMCA era. That is, post-DIDMCA, monetary policy seems to have a more lasting effect on RI.

The correlations among the contemporaneous innovations in the system's variable are shown in table 5.9 for the pre-83 sub-sample and in table 5.10 for the post-82 sub-sample. The contemporaneous effect of M_1 on RI is lower, but only slightly, in the post-DIDMCA era. The effect of M_1 on GNP, however, reverses to a negative sign in the post-DIDMCA era (from .38 to -.24). Surprisingly, the coefficient between RI and GNP is drastically lower post-82 (from .57 to .17).

Figure 5.4 plots the impulse response of RI to M_1 for the pre- and post-DIDMCA sub-samples. Although the effect of M_1 is initially stronger for the pre-83 sub-sample, in the post-82 plot it has a positive effect for all 8 quarters forecasted.

The next set of VARs contains the variables M_1, FHA, RI and GNP (in that order). The pre-83 variance decompositions of RI are shown in table 5.11 and those for the post-82 sub-sample in table 5.12. The introduction of an interest rate has again decreased the overall importance of money. The biggest change in money's importance, however, is from the pre- to the post-DIDMCA era. Over this period of time, money declined from explaining 19.25 percent of RI's forecast error variance to explaining less than 3.5 percent, on average, of this variance. Also, the explanatory strength of FHA over RI falls post-

Table 5.7 Variance Decomposition of RI Pre-1983

TRIANGULARIZATION	FORECAST HORIZON	PCT. OF FORECAST ERROR VARIANCE EXPLAINED BY		
		M1	RI	GNP
M1 RI GNP	2 quarters	36.7	62.4	0.9
	4 quarters	30.4	63.6	6.0
	6 quarters	25.0	56.5	18.5
	8 quarters	22.5	45.9	31.6

Table 5.8 Variance Decomposition of RI Post-1982

TRIANGULARIZATION	FORECAST HORIZON	PCT. OF FORECAST ERROR VARIANCE EXPLAINED BY		
		M1	RI	GNP
M1 RI GNP	2 quarters	26.0	65.9	8.1
	4 quarters	39.9	51.2	8.9
	6 quarters	42.3	46.4	11.3
	8 quarters	43.1	42.6	14.3

Table 5.9 Correlations of Contemporaneous Innovations Pre-1983

VARIABLES	M1	RI	GNP
M1	1.00	.	.
RI	0.59	1.00	.
GNP	0.38	0.57	1.00

Table 5.10 Correlations of Contemporaneous Innovations Post-1982

VARIABLES	M1	RI	GNP
M1	1.00	.	.
RI	0.50	1.00	.
GNP	-0.24	0.17	1.00

Table 5.11 Variance Decomposition of RI Pre-1983 For The System Including FHA

TRIANGULARIZATION	FORECAST HORIZON	PCT. OF FORECAST ERROR VARIANCE EXPLAINED BY			
		M1	FHA	RI	GNP
M1 FHA RI GNP	2 quarters	31.3	2.9	65.4	0.4
	4 quarters	19.1	29.3	49.6	2.0
	6 quarters	12.8	49.8	34.7	2.7
	8 quarters	13.8	54.5	28.1	3.6

Table 5.12 Variance Decomposition of RI Post-1982 For The System Including FHA

TRIANGULARIZATION	FORECAST HORIZON	PCT. OF FORECAST ERROR VARIANCE EXPLAINED BY			
		M1	FHA	RI	GNP
M1 FHA RI GNP	2 quarters	1.2	10.5	48.7	39.6
	4 quarters	3.8	16.2	19.4	60.6
	6 quarters	3.4	16.1	11.7	68.8
	8 quarters	5.0	12.6	8.6	73.8

DIDMCA. In the pre-83 sub-sample FHA explained 34 percent of RI, on average, while post-82 it explained just under 14 percent. This again strongly suggests that credit crunches have historically played a major role in determining RI but it also suggests that interest rates hold explanatory power over RI outside that which is lent to it by its coincidence with (or determination of) disintermediation. Although insignificant in the pre-DIDMCA era, GNP is the dominant explanatory variable for RI in the post-DIDMCA era within this system.

The contemporaneous correlations among innovations are shown in table 5.13 for the pre-83 sub-sample and in table 5.14 for the post-82 sub-sample. There are a number of interesting results printed here. For the 60-82 data set, the correlations between M_1 and both RI and GNP are large and positive. The correlation between these last two variables is also large and positive. The correlation between FHA and RI is negative for this sub-sample, but very small. For the 83.1-91.1 data set, however, the correlation between FHA and RI is large and positive while that between M_1 and FHA is large and negative. The correlation between M_1 and RI is much smaller in table 5.14 than in table 5.13 and that between M_1 and GNP reverses to a negative coefficient in table 5.14. Unlike in table 5.10, the contemporaneous correlation between the innovations in RI and GNP did not take a noticeable decline in the post-82 sub-sample.

Figure 5.5 has the impulse responses of RI to unanticipated shocks in FHA for the pre-83 and post-82 sub-samples. As in the variance decompositions, FHA proves to have a much stronger effect on RI in the pre-DIDMCA era. It retains a decisively negative effect, however, even in the post-82 plot.

It is questionable whether the end of 1982 is the proper date to split the data set for the two sub-sample VARs. If only financial deregulation is considered, however, that is probably the single best point in time. There is, though, another consideration. In the late 1970's and early 1980's, other sources of funds began to provide significant amounts of liquidity to the mortgage credit market. Therefore, in the early 1980's, regardless of the of the direction of the net flow of funds at S&Ls, potential home buyers still had funds available from non-bank sources. As an example, Friedman (1989) reports that government inaugurated agencies such as the Government National Mortgage Association, Federal National Mortgage Association and Federal Home Loan Mortgage Corporation supplied more than 50 percent of all funds granted for new mortgages in the years 1980-1988.

Table 5.13 Correlations of Contemporaneous Innovations Pre-1983 For The System Including FHA

VARIABLES	M1	FHA	RI	GNP
M1	1.00	.	.	.
FHA	0.03	1.00	.	.
RI	0.56	-0.01	1.00	.
GNP	0.48	0.07	0.58	1.00

Table 5.14 Correlations of Contemporaneous Innovations Post-1982 For The System Including FHA

VARIABLES	M1	FHA	RI	GNP
M1	1.00	.	.	.
FHA	-0.42	1.00	.	.
RI	0.07	0.41	1.00	.
GNP	-0.15	0.32	0.51	1.00

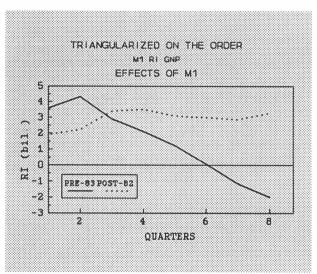

Figure 5.4 Impulse Response of RI to Innovations
in M1 Pre- and Post-DIDMCA

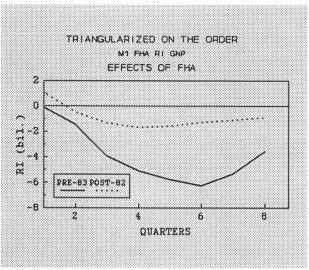

Figure 5.5 Impulse Response of RI to Innovations
in FHA Pre- and Post-DIDMCA

Further, of the total mortgage debt outstanding, 5.27 percent was held by the above agencies along with the Federal Housing Administration and Farmers Home Administration during the decade 1960-1969. Of the total mortgage debt outstanding 12.62 percent was held by these agencies in 1970-1979, 25.95 percent in 1980-1989 and 32 percent in 1990 (Economic Report Of The President, 1991). This is a competitive source of funds obtained by issuing debt securities in the open market based on approved mortgages and backed by the respective agency.

Because of this growth in the competitive market for mortgage funds, which coincided with the passage of DIDMCA, it may be that disintermediation lost its effect over RI at least one and maybe even two or three years before the first quarter of 1983. To investigate this possibility, VARs were run for a data set that included the years 1981.1-1991.1. The variables for this VAR were M_1, FHA, RI and GNP. The variance decomposition for RI under this system is shown in table 5.15. Here, although M_1 is still not very strong, FHA explains 35.2 percent of RI's forecast error variance.

As a final check of how sensitive the result of RI's responses to M_1 and FHA are to the break point in the data set, a VAR was run with a data set that included the years 1984.1-1991.1. For this system, money again becomes important. M_1 explained, on average, 17.6 percent of RI's forecast error variance and displayed a long term effect. FHA also was an important explanatory factor accounting for 32.9 percent, on average. The complete variance decomposition of RI for this system is shown in table 5.16. The two conclusions reached from table 5.15 are reaffirmed in table 5.16. That is, the interest rate still appears to be important in determining RI, and the specific results of the 'post-DIDMCA' VARs are not very robust to changes in the time periods included in the data set. Impulse responses are shown in figures 5.6 and 5.7 for the post-80 and post-84 samples.

Table 5.15 Variance Decomposition of RI Post-1980

TRIANGULARIZATION	FORECAST HORIZON	PCT. OF FORECAST ERROR VARIANCE EXPLAINED BY			
		M1	FHA	RI	GNP
M1 FHA RI GNP	2 quarters	0.1	24.6	73.3	2.0
	4 quarters	2.3	43.2	54.0	0.5
	6 quarters	6.1	39.8	51.0	3.1
	8 quarters	14.2	33.2	48.0	4.6

Table 5.16 Variance Decomposition of RI Post-1983

TRIANGULARIZATION	FORECAST HORIZON	PCT. OF FORECAST ERROR VARIANCE EXPLAINED BY			
		M1	FHA	RI	GNP
M1 FHA RI GNP	2 quarters	3.0	13.8	45.8	37.4
	4 quarters	16.6	43.8	11.9	27.7
	6 quarters	20.2	40.9	10.2	28.7
	8 quarters	30.4	33.1	8.2	28.3

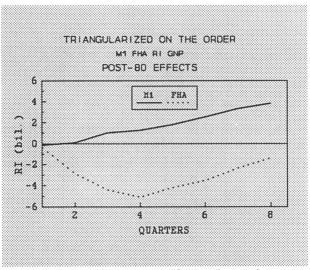

Figure 5.6 Impulse Response of RI to Innovations
in M1 and FHA Post-1980

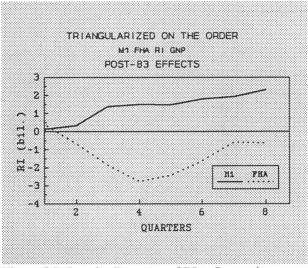

Figure 5.7 Impulse Response of RI to Innovations
in M1 and FHA Post-1983

VI

Conclusion

The study behind this book focused on an empirical examination of real residential fixed investment. The purpose was essentially twofold. The first objective was to examine the cyclical nature of RI while paying special attention to its relationships with monetary policy, inflation and interest rates. This research has brought the empirical knowledge concerning the cyclical behavior of RI up to the level currently known for other aggregate time series (such as gross national product, industrial production, consumption and business fixed investment). To do this, RI was studied using a statistical system akin to a simultaneous equations model (i.e. within a statistical technique which incorporated potential feedback and/or mutual causality among the variables in the system). Heretofore RI examinations have consisted almost exclusively of partial equilibrium demand functions (often in the form of demand functions for new housing). The second objective of the research was to consider the implications of these empirical results for the recent conclusions regarding the limited efficacy of monetary policy and the lack of causality from interest rates to fluctuations in real economic activity (e.g. Sims' theory of post-war business cycles and the Fama-Litterman-Weiss hypothesis).

As previously stated, these aforementioned theories began with Sims (1980b), who shows that money appears causally prior to output until a nominal interest rate is added to the system. After the inclusion of the nominal interest rate, it itself appears strongly causally prior and money loses its significance. Sims attributes this to the fact that money and output are both reacting to surprise changes in the interest rate. Money, however, reacts more quickly to the rate changes and so when the rate is excluded from consideration it looks like money causes output because its moves shortly and consistently lead the moves in output. Litterman and Weiss (1985) and Lawrence and Siow (1985) went a step further than Sims to show that even interest rates (real and nominal) possess no causality over output or business fixed investment. They break nominal interest rates down into two components - real rates and anticipated inflation. From this breakdown, they show that real rates have no significant explanatory power for output or BFI and that anticipated inflation holds almost as much explanatory power as do nominal rates. This last point suggests that nominal rates hold little predictive power for future output or BFI beyond that which is lent to them by their expected inflation component. Fama (1982) outlined the theory for which these empirical studies were providing statistical verification. His hypothesis is based on the tenet that, through the re-equilibration of actual and desired real money balances, output causes inflation. Therefore, anticipations about changes in future real output are reflected in anticipations about changes in future inflation. The anticipations about future real output changes are, however, not observable per se (to econometric investigators) but are tacit in the anticipated inflation changes indirectly observable in nominal interest rate movements. The statistical implications of causality of nominal interest rates and/or anticipated inflation over real output are theoretically removed by Fama's work.

The statistical procedure used to examine RI was vector autoregressions (VARs). Although controversial in some respects, VARs provided the best technique for the purposes here. First, they allow for the incorporation of possible bi-directional causality. Also, the Sims and Fama-Litterman-Weiss hypotheses were formulated and tested within VARs. The use of the technique here allows their results and the validity of their conclusions to be confronted directly.

The plan to use RI as a means to examine or re-examine trade cycle theories and thereby confront and/or change their conclusions needed to be justified. The contribution of this aspect of the study is the fact that RI is a leading aggregate economic time series, whereas the studies mentioned above have examined either coincidental (GNP and industrial production) or lagging series (BFI). If money and interest rates do affect the overall economy, it is realistic to expect that the transmission of the effect is through series that make their cyclical turns prior to those in the general business cycle. Therefore, if money and interest rates do affect the overall economy indirectly by way of residential investment, this effect may become obscured empirically unless it is individually and directly examined. Also deserving mention was the magnitude of RI in the business cycle, as this directly bears on its ability to act as a business cycle impulse mechanism. As discussed in chapter 1, RI has accounted for a 5.2 percent of GNP over the past four decades. At the height of its most pronounced cycles, however, RI has accounted for over 8.5 percent of GNP. At least as important as its size, RI's extreme relative volatility lends support and credibility to its role as a possible business cycle impulse.

Money was shown to have a moderate effect on RI until a long term nominal interest rate was considered (FHA). This result is similar to the finding of Sims. Unlike the findings of Litterman and Weiss, however, this research did not show that nominal interest rates hold predictive power for RI only through their expected inflation component (EINF). In fact, the nominal long term interest rate on FHA mortgages appears to hold substantial explanatory power over RI far beyond that lent to it by its inflation component. The finding of strong priorness of FHA to RI is robust through systems of different variables and through re-orderings within these systems. Likewise, RI was found to be strongly prior to GNP and this result was also extremely robust. These results lend support and provide credibility to a portion of the proposed causal business cycle chain set forth in this paper. This partial business cycle chain is from nominal interest rates through real residential investment to real GNP. These results run counter to propositions such as real business cycle theory, which asserts that nominal rates should play no causal role in real business cycles. The final results neither support nor condemn the monetarist theory of cycles.

Given the limited number of observations and the uncertainty of when the post-DIDMCA era actually began, the results for the changes in RI's behavior post-DIDMCA are only preliminary estimations. There are, however, two results from chapter 5 which can be stated with some certainty. First, prior to deregulation, the proxy used in this paper for credit crunches (GAP) is strongly causally prior to RI. This supports the proposition that, historically, high interest rate episodes have in part affected the level of RI through disintermediation. Also supported is the fact that in this era after financial deregulation, long term nominal interest rates are still causally prior to RI through the demand side of the market (although the magnitude of the effect is uncertain). There are a few other statistics from chapter 5 worthy of a final mention. In two of the sub-samples considered (1960.1-1982.4 and 1984.1-1991.1), M_1 appears causally prior to RI even in a system with a nominal interest rate. In both of these cases, M_1 explains approximately 19 percent of RI's forecast error variance, on average, over the 8 quarters forecasted. For the post-1982 contemporaneous innovation correlations (table 5.14, p.107), M_1 has a large negative coefficient with FHA (-.42). Finally, for the system of M_1, FHA, RI and GNP, the latter variable becomes important in RI explanation in both the post-82 and post-83 sub-samples. These last three results suggest that the nature of RI's behavior has changed somewhat after deregulation. The changes, however, may be different from what many had suspected. Depending on where the data sets were split, the more complete business cycle chain of M_1 to FHA through RI to GNP appears more strongly supported by the data in the post-DIDMCA era than it did pre-DIDMCA (even considering the result that FHA lost some of its effect on RI). Also, post DIDMCA, there appears to be a feedback between RI and GNP.

All of these last results mentioned are tentative and not robust. They do strongly suggest, though, that post-DIDMCA RI deserves further empirical consideration and should be examined in future business cycle research.

REFERENCES

Akhtar, M. A. and Ethan S. Harris (1987). "Monetary Policy
Influence on the Economy-an Empirical Analysis." Federal Reserve
Bank of New York, *Quarterly Review* (Winter), 19-34.

Barro, Robert J. and Herschel I. Grossman (1976). *Money,
Employment and Inflation*. Cambridge, MA: Cambridge
University Press.

Bernanke, B. (1983a). "The Determinants of Investment:
Another Look." *American Economic Review* 73, 71-75.

Bernanke, B. (1983b). "Irreversibility, Uncertainty and Cyclical
Investment." *Quarterly Journal of Economics* 98, 85-106.

Bernanke, B. and Alan S. Blinder (1992). "The Federal Funds Rate
And The Channels Of Monetary Transmission." *American Economic
Review* 82, 901-921.

Beveridge, Stephen and Charles R. Nelson (1981). "A New
Approach to Decomposition of Economic Time Series Into
Permanent and Transitory Components with Particular
Attention to Measurement of the 'Business Cycle'." *Journal of
Monetary Economics* 7, 151-174.

Blanchard, Olivier Jean and Stanley Fischer (1989). *Lectures On
Macroeconomics*. Cambridge, MA: MIT Press.

Boehm, Thomas P. and Joseph A. McKenzie (1981). "The
Investment Demand for Housing." Federal Home Loan Bank
Board Research Working Paper no. 99.

Business Conditions Digest. Various years and issues.

Chan, K. Hung, Jack C. Hayya, and J. Keith Ord (1977). "A
Note on Trend Removal Methods: The Case of Polynomial Versus
Variate Differencing." *Econometrica* 45, 737-744.

Clark, P. (1970). "Investment in the 1970s: Theory
Performance and Prediction." *Brookings Papers on Economic
Activity* 1, 73-113.

Dickey, David A. and Wayne A. Fuller (1979). "Distribution of the
Estimators for Autoregressive Time Series with a unit Root."
Journal of the American Statistical Association 74, 427-431.

Dickey, David A. and Wayne A. Fuller (1981). "Likelihood Ratio
Statistics for Autoregressive Time Series with a Unit Root."
Econometrica 49, 1057-1072.

117

Duca, John V. and Stuart S. Rosenthal (1991). "An Empirical Test of Credit Rationing in the Mortgage Market." *Journal of Urban Economics* 2, 218-234.

Economic Report of the President. (1991).

Eichenbaum, Martin and Kenneth J. Singleton (1986). "Do Equilibrium Real Business Cycle Theories Explain Postwar U.S. Business Cycles?" in *NBER Macroeconomics Annual 1986*, ed. Stanley Fischer, 1: 91-135. Cambridge, MA: MIT Press.

Eisner, R. (1978). *Factors in Business Investment*. Cambridge, MA: Ballinger.

Eisner, R. and R. I. Nadiri (1968). "Investment Behavior and Neoclassical Theory." *Review of Economic Activity* 1, 61-121.

Engle, Robert F. and C. W. J. Granger (1987). "Co-Integration and Error Correction: Representation, Estimation, and Testing." *Econometrica* 55, 251-276.

Fama, E. (1975). "Short-term Interest Rates as Predictors of Inflation." *American Economic Review* 65, 269-282.

Fama, E. (1982). "Inflation, Output, and Money." *The Journal of Business* 55, 201-231.

Fama, E. and M. Gibbons (1982). "Inflation, Real Returns, and Capital Investment." *Journal of Monetary Economics* 9, 297-323.

Federal Reserve Bulletin. Various years and issues.

Fisher, Irving (1923). "The Business Cycle Largely a 'Dance of the Dollar'." *Journal of the American Statistical Association* (December), 1024-1028.

Friedman, Benjamin M. (1986). "Money, Credit, and Interest Rates in the Business Cycle," in Robert J. Gordon (ed.), *The American Business Cycle*. Chicago, IL: The University of Chicago Press, 395-450.

Friedman, Benjamin M. (1989). "Effects of Monetary Policy on Real Economic Activity." Paper presented at symposium on Monetary Policy Issues in the 1990's sponsored by the Federal Reserve Bank of Kansas City, (September), 1-2.

Friedman, Milton (1961). "The Lag in Effect of Monetary Policy." *The Journal of Political Economy* 69, 447-466.

Friedman, Milton (1968). "The Role of Monetary Policy." *American Economic Review* 58, 1-17.

Friedman, Milton (1969). "The Supply of Money and Changes in Prices and Output," in *The Optimum Quantity of Money and Other Essays*. Chicago, IL: Aldine Publishing Company. 171-187.

Friedman, Milton, et al. (1974). *Milton Friedman's Monetary Framework: A Debate with His Critics*. Chicago, IL: University of Chicago Press.

Friedman, Milton and Anna J. Schwartz. (1963a). *A Monetary History of the United States*. Princeton, NJ: Princeton University Press.

Friedman, Milton and Anna J. Schwartz (1963b). "Money and Business Cycles." *Review of Economics and Statistics* 45, 32-64.

Friedman, Milton and Anna J. Schwartz (1991). "Alternative Approaches to Analyzing Economic Data." *The American Economic Review* 81, 39-49.

Follain, J. (1982). "Does Inflation Affect Real Behavior: The Case of Housing." *Southern Economic Journal* 48, 570-82.

Granger, C. W. J. (1969). "Investigating Causal Relations by Econometric Models and Cross-Spectral Methods." *Econometrica* 37, 424-438.

Granger, C. W. J. (1981). "Some Properties of Time Series Data and Their use in Econometrics Model Specification." *Journal of Econometrics* 121-130.

Grossman, S. and L. Weiss (1982). "Heterogenous Information and the Theory of the Business Cycle." *Journal of Political Economy* 90, 699-727.

Hakkio, Craig S. and Charles S. Morris (1984). "Vector Autoregressions: A User's Guide." Federal Reserve Bank of Kansas City, Research Working Paper.

Hall, R. (1977). "Investment, Interest Rates and Effects of Stabilization Policies." *Brookings Papers on Economic Activity* 1, 61-121.

Hendershott, P. (1980). "Real User Costs and the Demand for Single-Family Housing." *Brookings Papers on Economic Activity* 2, 401-444.

Hendershott, P. and J. Shilling (1982). "The Economics of Tenure Choice, 1955-1979," in *Research in Real Estate*. Jai Press, 105-134.

Jaffee, D. M. and K. Rosen (1979). "Mortgage Credit Availability and Residential Construction." *Brookings Papers on Economic Activity* 2, 333-376.

Johnston, J. (1984). *Econometric Methods*. 3rd ed. New York, NY: McGraw-Hill Book Company.

Kahn, George A. (1989). "The Changing Interest Sensitivity of the U.S. Economy." Federal Reserve Bank of Kansas City, *Economic Review* (November), 13-34.

Kashyap, Anil K., Jeremy C. Stein and David W. Wilcox (1993). "Monetary Policy And Credit Conditions: Evidence From The Composition Of External Finance." *American Economic Review* 83, 78-98.

Kearl, J. E. (1978). "Inflation, Mortgages, and Housing." *Journal of Political Economy* 82, 1115-38.

Kent, R. (1980). "Credit Rationing and the Home Mortgage Market." *Journal of Money, Credit and Banking* 12, 488-501.

Kydland, Finn E. and Edward C. Prescott (1990). "Business Cycles: Real Facts and a Monetary Myth." Federal Reserve Bank of Minneapolis, *Quarterly Review* (Spring), 3-18.

Lawrence, Colin and Aloysius Siow (1985). "Interest Rates and Investment Spending: Some Empirical Evidence for Postwar U.S. Producer Equipment, 1947-1980." *Journal of Business* 58, 359-375.

Litterman, Robert B. and Laurence Weiss (1985). "Money, Real Interest Rates, and Output: A Reinterpretation of Postwar U.S. Data." *Econometrica* 53, 129-156.

Lucas, Robert E. (1972). "Expectations and the Neutrality of Money." *Journal of Economic Theory* 4, 103-124.

Lucas, Robert E. (1973). "Some International Evidence on Output-Inflation Tradeoffs." *American Economic Review* 63, 326-334.

Lucas, Robert E. (1977). "Understanding Business Cycles," in Karl Brunner and Allan Meltzer (eds.), *Stabilization of the Domestic and International Economy*. Amsterdam: North-Holland, 7-29.

McCallum, Bennett T. (1983). "A reconsideration of Sims' Evidence Concerning Monetarism." *Economic Letters* 13, 167-171.

McCulloch, J. Huston (1975). "The Monte Carlo Cycle in Business Activity." *Economic Inquiry* 13, 303-321.

Mitchell, Wesley C. (1913). *Business Cycles*. Berkeley, CA: University of California Press.

Nelson, Charles R. and Heejoon Kang (1981). "Spurious Periodicity in Inappropriately Detrended Time Series." *Econometrica* 49, 741-751.

Nelson, Charles R. and Charles I. Plosser (1982). "Trends and Random Walks In Macroeconomic Time Series." *Journal of Monetary Economics* 10, 139-162.

Nelson, Charles R. and G. Schwert (1977). "Short-Term Interest Rates as Predictors of Inflation: On Testing the Hypothesis that the Real Rate of Interest os Constant." *American Economic Review* 67, 478-486.

Pankratz, Alan (1983). *Forecasting With Univariate Box-Jenkins Models.* New York, NY: John Wiley & Sons.

Pindyck, Robert S. and Daniel L. Rubinfeld (1991). *Econometric Models and Economic Forecasts.* 3 ed., New York, NY: McGraw-Hill, Inc.

Pozdena, Randall J. (1990). "Do Interest Rates Still Affect Housing." Federal Reserve Bank of San Francisco, *Economic Review* (Summer), 3-14.

Runkle, David E. (1987). "Vector Autoregressions and Reality." *Journal of Business and Economic Statistics* 5, 437-442.

Sargan, J. D. and A. Bhargava (1983). "Testing Residuals from Least Squares Regression for Being Generated by the Gaussion Random Walk." *Econometrica* 51, 153-174.

Schwab, R. (1982). "Inflation Expectation and the Demand for Housing." *American Economic Review* 72, 143-153.

Schwab, R. (1983). "Real and Nominal Interest Rates and the Demand for Housing." *Journal of Urban Economics* 13, 181-195.

Shapiro, Matthew D. (1986). "Investment, Output, and the Cost of Capital." *Brookings Papers on Economic Activity* 1, 111-152.

Shiller, R. J. (1979). "The Volatility of Long Term Interest Rates and Expectations Models of the Term Structure." *Journal of Political Economy* 87, 119-1219.

Shiller, R. J. (1980). "Can the Fed Control Real Interest Rates?" in *Rational Expectations and Economic Policy*, ed. by Stanley Fischer. Chicago, IL: University of Chicago Press.

Shiller, R. J. and J. Y. Campbell (1984). "A Simple Account of the Behavior of Long-Term Interest Rates." *American Economic Review* 74, 44-48.

Sims, Christopher A. (1972). "Money, Income, and Causality." *American Economic Review* 62, 540-552.

Sims, Christopher, A. (1980a). "Macroeconomics and Reality." *Econometrica* 48, 1-48.

Sims, Christopher, A. (1980b). "Comparison of Interwar and
    Postwar Business Cycles: Monetarism Reconsidered." *American
    Economic Review* 70, 250-257.
Sims, Christopher, A. (1981). "An Autoregressive Index Model for
    the U.S., 1948-1975," in *Large-Scale Macro-Econometric Models*,
    ed. by J. Kmenta and J. B. Ramsey. Amsterdam: North-Holland
    Publishing Co.
Sims, Christopher, A. (1987). "Comment." *Journal of Business
    and Economic Statistics* 5, 443-449.
Spencer, David E. (1989). "Does Money Matter? The Robustness
    of Evidence From Vector Autoregressions." *Journal of Money,
    Credit, and Banking* 21, 442-454.
Survey of Current Business. Various years and issues.
Todd, Richard M. (1990). "Vector Autoregressive Evidence on
    Monetarism: Another Look at the Robustness Debate." Federal
    Reserve Bank of Minneapolis *Quarterly Review* (Spring), 19-37.
Van Order, Robert and Ann Dougherty (1991). "Housing Demand
    and Real Interest Rates." *Journal of Urban Economics* 2, 191-201.

INDEX